Brain Quest

Dear Parent,

"It's Fun to Be Smart!" That's not just our slogan, it's our philosophy. For over twenty years we've been adding a big dose of "fun" to learning—first with our bestselling Q&A Brain Quest card decks; then with all the licensed games and products bearing the Brain Quest brand; and, of course, with Brain Quest Workbooks.

At Brain Quest we believe:

- All kids are smart—though they learn at their own speed.

- All kids learn best when they're having fun.

- All kids deserve the chance to reach their potential—given the tools they need, there's no limit to how far they can go!

Brain Quest Workbooks are the perfect tools to help children get a leg up in all areas of curriculum; they can hone their reading skills or dig in with math drills, review the basics or get a preview of lessons to come. These are not textbooks, but rather true workbooks—best used as supplements to what kids are learning in school, reinforcing curricular concepts while encouraging creative problem solving and higher-level thinking. You and your child can tackle a page or two a day—or an entire chapter over the course of a long holiday break. Your child will be getting great help with basic schoolwork, and you will be better able to gauge how well he or she is understanding basic course material.

Each Brain Quest Workbook has been written in consultation with an award-winning educator specializing in that grade, and is compliant with most school curricula across the country. We cover the core competencies of reading, writing, and math in depth—with chapters on science, social studies, and other popular units rounding out the curriculum. Easy-to-navigate pages with color-coded tabs help identify chapters, while Brain Boxes offer parent-friendly explanations of key concepts and study units. That means parents can use the workbooks in conjunction with what their children are learning in school, or to explain material in ways that are consistent with current teaching strategies. In either case, the workbooks create an important bridge to the classroom, an effective tool for parents, homeschoolers, tutors, and teachers alike.

Learning is an adventure—a quest for knowledge. At Brain Quest we strive to guide children on that quest, to keep them motivated and curious, and to give them the confidence they need to do well in school . . . and beyond. We're confident that Brain Quest Workbooks will play an integral role in your child's adventure. So let the learning—and the fun—begin!

—The editors of Brain Quest

This book belongs to:

Workbook series design by Raquel Jaramillo
Illustrations by Nick Thornborrow and Matt Rockefeller

Workman books are available at special discounts when purchased in bulk for premiums and sales promotions as well as for fund-raising or educational use. Special editions or book excerpts can also be created to specification. For details, contact the Special Sales Director at the address below, or send an email to specialmarkets@workman.com.

Workman Publishing Co., Inc.
225 Varick Street
New York, NY 10014-4381
workman.com

Printed in the United States of America
First printing April 2015

10 9 8 7 6

Brain Quest
Grade 6
Workbook

Written by Persephone Walker
Consulting Editor: Ryan Vernosh

WORKMAN PUBLISHING
NEW YORK

4

Contents

5

Spelling and Vocabulary

Gumdrops and Jawbreakers

Read the story. Circle the **soft g** and **hard g** words. Then sort them in the jars below.

"Gumdrops," said Genevieve.

"Jawbreakers," said Gus.

"Just a minute now," said Jerry, who stood behind the rows of jars filled with chewing gum and nougat. "You only have enough for one or the other."

"Jawbreakers are giant," Gus argued.

"Gumdrops are gooey."

They looked at Jerry. "Don't ask me," he said. "I'm not one to judge." But then he grinned and pulled out a bunch of green grapes. "Personally, I think these are great."

"They're not giant," Genevieve said, "or gooey."

"It doesn't matter," said Jerry. "They're good."

Brain Box

The **soft g** can be spelled **j**, **g**, or **dge**.

At the beginning of a syllable, it is spelled **j** or **g**.

At the end of a syllable, it is spelled **ge** or **dge**.

Here is an exception: It is also spelled with a **g** when followed by **g** or **y**.

JAWBREAKERS SOFT G

GUMDROPS HARD G

The Magic Suffix

Finish each sentence by changing the verb into a noun. Add the **suffix** -ance or -ence.

Can someone assist me, please? I need some _assistance_.

Carol couldn't attend class, so she lost points for _attendance_.

No one could understand why the old man would just disappear without warning. For years, everyone in town talked about his _disappear_.

She loved to perform, and she loved all the excitement that led up to a _performence_.

The two paintings didn't seem to differ, but the expert claimed there was a clear _differance_.

No matter what happened, she had the grit to persist, and eventually her _persistence_ paid off.

BONUS:

The puppy came up with endless ways to disobey, but he was so cute no one could stay angry over his _____.

Brain Box

A **suffix** comes at the end of a word and changes the word's meaning.

A verb can be changed to a noun by adding the suffix **-ance** or **-ence**.

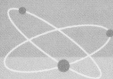

Homophones

Complete each sentence with one of the following pairs of **homophones**.

hour	our		waste	waist
writes	rights		days	daze
rain	reign		they're	there
allowed	aloud		sail	sale

After dinner, we were _____ to read _____.

"_____ right _____!" she said, pointing to the books.

In the Declaration of Independence, Thomas Jefferson _____ about our _____ .

Everything seemed to be changing so fast that she spent the next few _____ in a _____.

Because the king angered the old wizard, the wizard declared it would _____ for the rest of the king's _____.

It seemed like a _____ to throw the old ribbon away, so she tied it around her _____.

He finally learned to _____ after they bought a boat on _____.

If you drive for another _____, you'll arrive at _____ house.

Double Vision

Add the appropriate suffix to each word, and double the final consonant when necessary.

Add "ing"		Add "ed"	
forget	_____	scar	_____
wonder	_____	boost	_____
fit	_____	map	_____
admit	_____	jump	_____
knit	_____	fan	_____
plot	_____	slip	_____
listen	_____	play	_____
excel	_____	crunch	_____

Brain Box

Sometimes the **final consonant** is doubled before adding the **suffix**.

When the root word has one short vowel and one final consonant, the final consonant needs to be doubled before adding the suffix.

In the Beginning

Complete each sentence with the proper **prefix**.

It was a major _____ duction every time Sherlock came up with another _____ duction.

He worked hard to get his _____ motion, but he worked even harder to make sure he didn't get a _____ motion.

When she took the throne, the queen _____ nounced a pardon for all the subjects the evil prime minister had unfairly _____ nounced.

He sent a _____ fuse apology, in hopes that he could _____ fuse the situation.

Just as the client was being _____ posed, the lovesick lawyer fell to one knee and _____ posed.

Brain Box

A **prefix** is a word segment that changes the meaning of a word when added to the beginning.

The prefix **pro-** means "before" or "forward." It can also mean "to show support."

The prefix **de-** means "from" or "away." It can also mean "to reverse" or "undo" something.

Not!

Add **in-**, **il-**, **ir-**, or **im-** to each word to make each word mean the opposite.

___ability

___legal

___regular

___permanent

___equity

___polite

___legible

___possible

___capable

___patient

___complete

___logical

___formal

___responsible

___action

___purity

Spelling and Vocabulary

Prefixes

Brain Box

The prefixes **in-**, **il-**, **ir-**, and **im-** mean "not." Adding any of these prefixes to a word will make the word mean the opposite.

Spelling and Vocabulary

Spelling

Tricky Words

Choose the correct spelling of each tricky vocabulary word. Then find the correctly spelled words in the word search on the facing page. The words may go across or down.

ekonomic / economic / economik

atmosphere / atmosfere / atmosfear

circumfrence / circumfirence / circumference

parralel / parallel / paralell

encyclopedia / inyclopedia / encyklopedea

individgual / individual / indevidual

metafor / metaphor / metephor

virus / vyrus / virrus

arkeologist / arceologist / archaeologist

boundiry / boundary / boundery

H	F	W	U	J	A	V	Q	B	Q	L	X	M	G	M	D	N	J	B	D	T	Q
U	C	A	L	Q	R	D	X	R	D	Q	F	B	O	U	N	D	A	R	Y	P	S
T	N	U	K	C	C	F	Z	F	E	P	R	A	A	D	G	E	J	W	L	Q	W
V	H	Y	K	D	H	E	H	P	C	Z	Y	H	C	I	Y	R	R	N	V	H	K
H	N	K	D	M	A	C	G	W	V	I	R	U	S	F	M	C	H	D	H	E	A
P	K	X	P	I	E	O	K	R	U	R	Q	U	E	Y	B	H	W	T	L	N	M
E	S	C	A	A	O	N	Z	S	L	B	V	H	R	Y	O	A	W	M	A	C	E
N	Z	V	R	P	L	O	L	U	T	I	O	N	R	V	U	N	T	U	P	Y	T
T	C	B	A	A	O	M	D	I	I	B	J	H	H	Y	N	D	B	Y	P	C	A
H	P	I	L	J	G	I	J	Y	P	K	O	T	N	A	D	I	Y	R	R	L	P
O	H	Y	L	I	I	C	E	N	L	C	L	J	S	N	A	S	C	W	O	O	H
U	N	C	E	K	S	A	V	V	Y	Q	X	C	C	X	R	E	P	K	X	P	O
S	U	Q	L	A	T	E	K	H	W	A	T	M	O	S	P	H	E	R	E	E	R
E	I	I	N	D	I	V	I	D	U	A	L	D	T	O	E	T	A	O	M	D	O
U	C	I	R	C	U	M	F	E	R	E	N	C	E	U	S	J	Y	K	A	I	P
E	I	V	V	O	P	L	T	O	G	L	M	N	A	S	R	I	C	S	T	A	L
J	H	J	A	D	L	A	J	A	V	E	L	I	N	F	W	T	U	A	E	A	A

Can you find the bonus words? Write them here.

_____

_____

_____

Exactly!

Good writers don't just use any word. They use the **exact word**.

Connect each word on the left with its more specific version on the right by drawing a line between them.

water	deck hand
blue	schooner
boat	cirrus
cloud	ocean
fish	indigo
sailor	gusts
wind	swells
waves	marlin
storm	typhoon

Literature Comprehension

The Facts of the Matter

Read this excerpt from Henry Wadsworth Longfellow's poem "Paul Revere's Ride."

Paul Revere's Ride

Listen, my children, and you shall hear
Of the midnight ride of Paul Revere,
On the eighteenth of April, in Seventy-five;
Hardly a man is now alive
Who remembers that famous day and year.
He said to his friend, "If the British march
By land or sea from the town to-night,
Hang a lantern aloft in the belfry arch
Of the North Church tower as a signal light,—
One, if by land, and two, if by sea;
And I on the opposite shore will be,
Ready to ride and spread the alarm
Through every Middlesex village and farm,
For the country-folk to be up and to arm."

Brain Box

Textual evidence is all the information gathered from reading a text.

Explicit evidence is clearly stated in the text.

Draw **inferences** by forming logical conclusions about the facts in the text.

What happens in this excerpt? Write down all the facts.

_____   _____
_____   _____
_____   _____
_____   _____
_____   _____

What can you infer from the facts in the text?

_____
_____
_____
_____
_____
_____
_____

Poetry and Prose

Rewrite Longfellow's poem about Paul Revere as a story. Include as many of the **facts** and **details** as possible.

Literature Comprehension

Textual evidence

Paul Revere's Ride

_____

_____

_____

_____

_____

_____

_____

_____

_____

_____

_____

_____

_____

_____

_____

_____

_____

_____

_____

_____

How does rewriting the poem as a story change how you read it?

_____

_____

_____

_____

Brain Box

Some poems use **rhyme**, **rhythm**, **meter**, and more fanciful language than prose.

The Main Theme

Read this excerpt from Mark Twain's *The Adventures of Tom Sawyer*. Tom is whitewashing a fence when his friend Ben, who is enjoying an apple, arrives.

Literature Comprehension

Themes

The Adventures of Tom Sawyer

Tom went on whitewashing. . . . Ben stared a moment and then said: "Hi-YI! YOU'RE up a stump, ain't you!"

No answer. Tom surveyed his last touch with the eye of an artist, then he gave his brush another gentle sweep and surveyed the result, as before. Ben ranged up alongside of him. Tom's mouth watered for the apple, but he stuck to his work. Ben said:

"Hello, old chap, you got to work, hey?"

Tom wheeled suddenly and said:

"Why, it's you, Ben! I warn't noticing."

"Say—I'm going in a-swimming, I am. Don't you wish you could? But of course you'd druther WORK—wouldn't you? Course you would!"

Tom contemplated the boy a bit, and said:

"What do you call work?"

"Why, ain't THAT work?"

Tom resumed his whitewashing, and answered carelessly:

"Well, maybe it is, and maybe it ain't. All I know, is, it suits Tom Sawyer."

"Oh come, now, you don't mean to let on that you LIKE it?"

The brush continued to move.

"Like it? Well, I don't see why I oughtn't to like it. Does a boy get a chance to whitewash a fence every day?"

That put the thing in a new light. Ben stopped nibbling his apple. Tom swept his brush daintily back and forth—stepped back to note the effect—added a touch here and there—criticized the effect again—Ben watching every move and getting more and more interested, more and more absorbed. Presently he said:

"Say, Tom, let ME whitewash a little."

Brain Box

The **theme** is the central idea the writer is interested in or wants to convey.

This conversation seems to be about painting a fence. But what larger theme is actually being discussed?

_____

What clues does the text give about this larger theme?

_____

_____

What points does the story seem to be making about this theme?

_____

_____

No Judgment

Write a summary of the exchange between Tom and Ben. Include all the facts, in chronological order, but be sure to leave out any of your own opinions.

Brain Box

To form strong **arguments**, you need to support them with facts. To see the events clearly, you need to look at them first without judgment. **Chronological order** organizes events according to the order in which they happen.

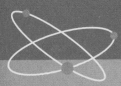

A Matter of Character

What do you learn about Tom and Ben in the course of their conversation?

The Bare Facts

List all the facts about Tom and Ben from their conversation.

TOM	BEN

The Logical Conclusions

Based on the facts, list all the logical conclusions, or **inferences**, you can make about what Tom and Ben are like.

TOM	BEN

Do either Tom or Ben change during the course of the conversation? How?

_____
_____
_____
_____

Literature Comprehension

Inferences and character

Brain Box

A **character** is a person in a story. **Character** can also mean the qualities that make you who you are. The things that happen to you and the choices you make all shape your character.

A Single Element

Sometimes an element in a story can be just as important as one of the characters. Along with Tom and Ben, the picket fence plays a big role in the story.

List all the times the fence is mentioned in the story. _____

_____

What kind of language is used when the fence is mentioned? Are there any themes that recur?

_____

_____

How does the language Mark Twain uses to describe the fence affect the rest of the story? _____

_____

What does Ben think of the fence? _____

_____

What does Tom think of the fence? _____

_____

How do Tom's actions reflect his thoughts? _____

_____

What do we learn about Tom from his interaction with the fence?

_____

Does the role of the fence change during the course of the story? If so, how?

_____

Does the fence seem to stand for anything but itself? If so, what?

_____

Brain Box

A **symbol** is a word or image that stands for something else. For example, a flag can stand for a country and a heart can stand for love.

A Change in Plans

Pretend you are a part of the scene in the excerpt below.
It describes a Christmas celebration in *Little Women*, by Louisa May Alcott.

Little Women

"Merry Christmas, little daughters! I'm glad you began at once, and hope you will keep on. But I want to say one word before we sit down. Not far away from here lies a poor woman with a little newborn baby. Six children are huddled into one bed to keep from freezing, for they have no fire. There is nothing to eat over there, and the oldest boy came to tell me they were suffering hunger and cold. My girls, will you give them your breakfast as a Christmas present?"

They were all unusually hungry, having waited nearly an hour, and for a minute no one spoke, only a minute, for Jo exclaimed impetuously, "I'm so glad you came before we began!"

"May I go and help carry the things to the poor little children?" asked Beth eagerly.

"I shall take the cream and the muffins," added Amy, heroically giving up the article she most liked.

Meg was already covering the buckwheats, and piling the bread into one big plate.

"I thought you'd do it," said Mrs. March, smiling as if satisfied. "You shall all go and help me, and when we come back we will have bread and milk for breakfast, and make it up at dinnertime."

They were soon ready, and the procession set out. Fortunately it was early, and they went through back streets, so few people saw them, and no one laughed at the queer party.

A poor, bare, miserable room it was, with broken windows, no fire, ragged bedclothes, a sick mother, wailing baby, and a group of pale, hungry children cuddled under one old quilt, trying to keep warm.

How the big eyes stared and the blue lips smiled as the girls went in.

"*Ach, mein Gott!* It is good angels come to us!" said the poor woman, crying for joy.

"Funny angels in hoods and mittens," said Jo, and set them to laughing.

In a few minutes it really did seem as if kind spirits had been at work there. Hannah, who had carried wood, made a fire, and stopped up the broken panes with old hats and her own cloak. Mrs. March gave the mother tea and gruel, and comforted her with promises of help, while she dressed the little baby as tenderly as if it had been her own. The girls meantime spread the table, set the children round the fire, and fed them like so many hungry birds, laughing, talking, and trying to understand the funny broken English.

"*Das ist gut!*" "*Die Engel-kinder!*" cried the poor things as they ate and warmed their purple hands at the comfortable blaze. The girls had never been called angel children before, and thought it very agreeable, especially Jo, who had been considered a Sancho" ever since she was born. That was a very happy breakfast, though they didn't get any of it. And when they went away, leaving comfort behind, I think there were not in all the city four merrier people than the hungry little girls who gave away their breakfasts and contented themselves with bread and milk on Christmas morning.

"That's loving our neighbor better than ourselves, and I like it," said Meg, as they set out their presents while their mother was upstairs collecting clothes for the poor Hummels.

This story describes a change in plans. But it's not just the plans that change—the characters do, too. Answer these questions.

What do the characters expect at the beginning of the story? How do those expectations change?

_____

_____

How does the change in plans reveal Amy's character?

_____

_____

How does the change in plans reveal Jo's character?

_____

_____

The German mother describes the girls as good angels. This is a change from the way Jo is usually seen. How is it different?

_____

_____

What do the characters get at the end of the story? How is it different from what they expected?

_____

_____

How does the difference between what the characters expected and what they got change them?

_____

_____

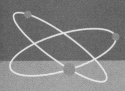
Clues in Context

The excerpt from *Little Women* (on page 22) contains several phrases that are not in standard English: Some are in old-fashioned slang, and some are in another language, German.

Use **context clues** to guess what the phrases below might mean.

Die Engel-kinder

Does *Engel-kinder* seem to be a positive or a negative term? Why?

_____

_____

What other clues does the text give to what *Engel-kinder* might mean?

_____

_____

Sancho

Does *Sancho* seem to be a positive or a negative term? Why?

_____

_____

What other clues does the text give to what *Sancho* might mean?

_____

_____

_____

_____

_____

_____

Brain Box

Context
refers to the surroundings of an unknown word or phrase. When you are not sure what a word means, you can take a guess by using the context clues that surround the word.

Dear March!

Write your own holiday story. Include characters and a plot that reveals characteristics about them.

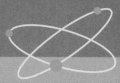

Literature Comprehension

Context clues

Cracking the Code

In his poem "Jabberwocky," Lewis Carroll includes dozens of made-up words. Even though none of those words are in a dictionary, you can still guess their meaning from **context**.

Jabberwocky

'Twas brillig, and the slithy toves
Did gyre and gimble in the wabe;
All mimsy were the borogoves,
And the mome raths outgrabe.

"Beware the Jabberwock, my son!
The jaws that bite, the claws that catch!
Beware the Jubjub bird, and shun
The frumious Bandersnatch!"

He took his vorpal sword in hand:
Long time the manxome foe he sought
So rested he by the Tumtum tree,
And stood awhile in thought.

And as in uffish thought he stood,
The Jabberwock, with eyes of flame,
Came whiffling through the tulgey wood,
And burbled as it came!

One, two! One, two! And through and through
The vorpal blade went snicker-snack!
He left it dead, and with its head
He went galumphing back.

"And hast thou slain the Jabberwock?
Come to my arms, my beamish boy!
O frabjous day! Callooh! Callay!"
He chortled in his joy.

'Twas brillig, and the slithy toves
Did gyre and gimble in the wabe;
All mimsy were the borogoves,
And the mome raths outgrabe.

Write your own definitions of Carroll's made-up words below. List the clues that helped you arrive at your conclusions. If there's just not enough evidence, write "no evidence."

Jabberwock

definition: _____

clues: _____

galumphing

definition: _____

clues: _____

vorpal

definition: _____

clues: _____

frumious

definition: _____

clues: _____

borogoves

definition: _____

clues: _____

frabjous

definition: _____

clues: _____

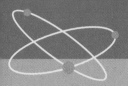

The Full Report

Rewrite the story told in "Jabberwocky" as if it were the front-page article in a newspaper. Make all the context clues explicit.

Jabberwocky: The Sequel

For each part of speech, make up your own word with a definition. Your fifth word can be whatever part of speech you choose.

noun: _____

verb: _____

adjective: _____

adverb: _____

_____: _____

Literature Comprehension

Parts of speech

Brain Box

A **noun** names a person, place, or thing.

A **verb** describes an action or a state of being.

An **adjective** describes a noun.

An **adverb** describes a verb or an adjective.

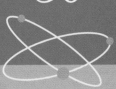

Books vs. TV

"Jabberwocky" is an adventure poem. Many TV shows are adventures, too. Books offer some things that shows do not, and shows offer some things that books do not.

What are three things that you get from a book that you can't get from a TV show?

_____

What are three things that you get from a TV show that you can't get from a book?

_____

What do you like better about TV shows than books?

_____

Have you ever read a book and then seen a show based on it, or seen a show and then read the book? How were the two different?

_____

What did the TV show do better than the book?

_____

What did the book do better than the TV show?

_____

Which did you prefer?

_____

See What?

Imagine that you are part of the scene in the opening chapter of *Treasure Island*, by Robert Louis Stevenson. A mysterious stranger arrives at a seaside inn. Read the passage and answer the questions that follow.

"The Old Sea-dog at the Admiral Benbow"

Squire Trelawney, Dr. Livesey, and the rest of these gentlemen having asked me to write down the whole particulars about Treasure Island, from the beginning to the end, keeping nothing back but the bearings of the island, and that only because there is still treasure not yet lifted, I take up my pen in the year of grace 17__ and go back to the time when my father kept the Admiral Benbow inn and the brown old seaman with the sabre cut first took up his lodging under our roof.

I remember him as if it were yesterday, as he came plodding to the inn door, his sea-chest following behind him in a hand-barrow—a tall, strong, heavy, nut-brown man, his tarry pigtail falling over the shoulder of his soiled blue coat, his hands ragged and scarred, with black, broken nails, and the sabre cut across one cheek, a dirty, livid white. I remember him looking round the cover and whistling to himself as he did so, and then breaking out in that old sea-song that he sang so often afterwards:

"Fifteen men on the dead man's chest—
Yo-ho-ho, and a bottle of rum!"

in the high, old tottering voice that seemed to have been tuned and broken at the capstan bars. Then he rapped on the door with a bit of stick like a handspike that he carried, and when my father appeared, called roughly for a glass of rum. This, when it was brought to him, he drank slowly, like a connoisseur, lingering on the taste and still looking about him at the cliffs and up at our signboard.

"This is a handy cove," says he at length; "and a pleasant sittyated grog-shop. Much company, mate?"

My father told him no, very little company, the more was the pity.

"Well, then," said he, "this is the berth for me. Here you, matey," he cried to the man who trundled the barrow; "bring up alongside and help up my chest. I'll stay here a bit," he continued. "I'm a plain man; rum and bacon and eggs is what I want, and that head up there for to watch ships off. What you mought call me? You mought call me captain. Oh, I see what you're at—there"; and he threw down three or four gold pieces on the threshold. "You can tell me when I've worked through that," says he, looking as fierce as a commander.

And indeed bad as his clothes were and coarsely as he spoke, he had none of the appearance of a man who sailed before the mast, but seemed like a mate or skipper accustomed to be obeyed or to strike. The man who came with the barrow told us the mail had set him down the morning before at the Royal George, that he had inquired what inns there were along the coast, and hearing ours well spoken of, I suppose, and described as lonely, had chosen it from the others for his place of residence. And that was all we could learn of our guest.

Who tells this story? What facts can we learn about the narrator? List at least five facts.

_____

_____

What kinds of things does the narrator notice about the new guest? List at least five things.

_____

_____

How does the narrator seem to feel about the guest? List at least three details, and what they reveal about the narrator's feelings toward the guest.

_____

_____

_____

What can we learn about the narrator from the way the narrator describes the guest? What does the narrator seem to be most interested in? What does that tell us about the narrator?

_____

_____

_____

_____

Brain Box

Perspective is a person's point of view. An author develops a character's perspective by carefully choosing details to emphasize. You gain clues to a character's point of view by paying close attention to those details.

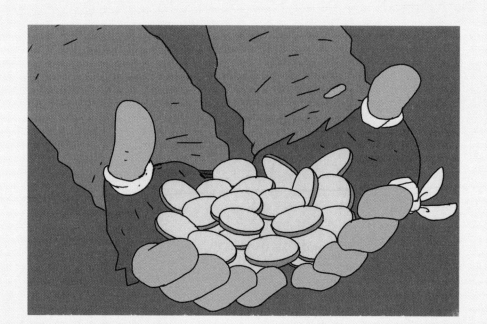

A Difference of Perspective

The strange guest and the innkeeper have a **difference of perspective** in this story when they discuss the amount of "company" at the inn.

What is the innkeeper's perspective on the number of guests at his inn?

_____

_____

_____

What is the guest's perspective?

_____

_____

_____

Why do you think the innkeeper might feel the way he does about the small number of guests?

_____

_____

_____

Why do you think the guest might feel the way he does?

_____

_____

_____

_____

_____

_____

ADMIRAL BENBOW INN

VACANCY

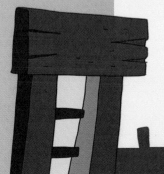

Another Difference

There is another difference of perspective in the story: The narrator was young when the events happened, but now remembers it as an adult.

What details in the story show that the narrator is now an adult? List three details.

_____

_____

What details in the story show that the narrator was a child when the events occurred? List three details.

_____

_____

Sometimes when we look back on events that happened earlier in our lives, we have a different perspective now than we had then. Do you see any places where that seems to be true in this story?

_____

_____

Look closely at the description of the new guest. List one description that seems to be from the perspective of a child, and explain why you believe it sounds like a child's perspective.

_____

_____

_____

List one description that seems to be from the perspective of an adult, and explain why you believe it sounds like an adult's perspective.

_____

_____

_____

Writing Your Own Narrative

Rewrite this scene from the **perspective** of one of the other characters, either the innkeeper or the strange guest. Use all the same events, but make up your own details to change the perspective.

Literature Comprehension

Perspective

(lined writing space)

Using clues from the scene, imagine how another character might have a point of view different from the narrator's.

What would another character notice that the narrator didn't?

_____

_____

How would another character's thoughts and feelings be different from the narrator's?

_____

_____

A Sea Shanty

The strange guest sings a song that begins:

> "Fifteen men on the dead man's chest—
> Yo-ho-ho, and a bottle of rum!"

Beginning with those two lines, finish the song with at least another ten lines.

Literature Comprehension

Perspective

Just the Facts

In H. G. Wells's *War of the Worlds*, a man takes an early-morning walk to look for a meteorite. Instead, he discovers a Martian spaceship. Imagine that you go along on this walk.

The Thing itself lay almost entirely buried in sand, amidst the scattered splinters of a fir tree it had shivered to fragments in its descent. The uncovered part had the appearance of a huge cylinder, caked over and its outline softened by a thick scaly dun-colored incrustation. It had a diameter of about thirty yards. He approached the mass, surprised at the size and more so at the shape, since most meteorites are rounded more or less completely. It was, however, still so hot from its flight through the air as to forbid his near approach. A stirring noise within its cylinder he ascribed to the unequal cooling of its surface; for at that time it had not occurred to him that it might be hollow.

He remained standing at the edge of the pit that the Thing had made for itself, staring at its strange appearance, astonished chiefly at its unusual shape and color, and dimly perceiving even then some evidence of design in its arrival. The early morning was wonderfully still, and the sun, just clearing the pine trees toward Weybridge, was already warm. He did not remember hearing any birds that morning, there was certainly no breeze stirring, and the only sounds were the faint movements from within the cindery cylinder. He was all alone on the common.

Then suddenly he noticed with a start that some of the gray clinker, the ashy incrustation that covered the meteorite, was falling off the circular edge of the end. It was dropping off in flakes and raining down upon the sand. A large piece suddenly came off and fell with a sharp noise that brought his heart into his mouth.

For a minute he scarcely realized what this meant, and, although the heat was excessive, he clambered down into the pit close to the bulk to see the Thing more clearly. He fancied even then that the cooling of the body might account for this, but what disturbed that idea was the fact that the ash was falling only from the end of the cylinder.

And then he perceived that, very slowly, the circular top of the cylinder was rotating on its body. It was such a gradual movement that he discovered it only through noticing that a black mark that had been near him five minutes ago was now at the other side of the circumference. Even then he scarcely understood what this indicated, until he heard a muffled grating sound and saw the black mark jerk forward an inch or so. Then the thing came upon him in a flash. The cylinder was artificial—hollow—with an end that screwed out! Something within the cylinder was unscrewing the top!

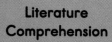

H. G. Wells's description gives us a good sense of what it might feel like to discover a spaceship on a morning walk. He even chooses to present his details so that you're just as confused as you might have been if you were there. But what really happens in this story?

Write a police report based on the events Wells depicts. Stick to the facts, and leave out feelings and guesses.

Police Report

Time of Day:

Location:

Description of the Thing:

The Events:

Brain Box

Details
refer to the particular information that an author chooses to describe in order to set a scene.

The details you choose to focus on can change the tone, or the general feeling, of a piece of writing.

Extra! Extra!

Pretty soon, news of a crashed spaceship will spread. And the facts probably won't stay as dry as they might be in a police report.

Write a version of the story as if you're trying to sell as many copies of a newspaper as possible. Use the facts, but make them as interesting as possible. Feel free to make crazy guesses and draw wild conclusions about what the facts might mean.

Brain Box

An author's **choice of details** doesn't just affect tone.

Depending on what details an author chooses to hide or reveal, the meaning of a piece of writing can change.

A Figure of Speech

Wells's story doesn't read like a police report or a tabloid article. His words were carefully chosen to set a mood. Read the following lines and answer the questions about why you think Wells chose the words he did.

"The Thing itself lay almost entirely buried in sand, amidst the scattered splinters of a fir tree it had shivered to fragments in its descent."

a) What is the simplest way to say what Wells describes here?

_____

b) What kind of image or mood is created by the use of the word *shivered*?

_____

"It was, however, still so hot from its flight through the air as to forbid his near approach."

a) What is the simplest way to say what Wells describes here?

_____

b) What kind of image or mood is created by the use of the word *forbid*?

_____

"It was dropping off in flakes and raining down upon the sand."

a) What is the simplest way to say what Wells describes here?

_____

b) What kind of image or mood is created by the use of the word *raining*?

_____

"A large piece suddenly came off and fell with a sharp noise that brought his heart into his mouth."

a) What is the simplest way to say what Wells describes here?

_____

b) What kind of image or mood is created by the use of the phrase "brought his heart into his mouth"?

_____

Brain Box

A **figure of speech** is a word or a phrase that says more than its literal meaning by implying a different or additional idea.

A Question of Perspective

There is one major character in this story whom you never get to see: the Martian in the spaceship. But the Martian has a side of the story, or perspective, too.

Rewrite this story as if you were the Martian, in the **first person**. What would you do if your ship crash-landed on another planet? How would you feel? What would you be thinking as you were just about to step out into a new world?

Brain Box

In **first-person** storytelling, the author uses "I" and "we."

In **second-person** storytelling, the author uses "you."

In **third-person** storytelling, the author uses "he," "she," "it," and "them." Other third-person pronouns are "him," "her," "they," and "their."

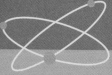

A Change in the Air

Read this excerpt from Frances Hodgson Burnett's *The Secret Garden* and go exploring with Mary as she investigates the gardens at her mysterious new home.

 The Secret Garden

She walked back into the first kitchen-garden she had entered and found the old man digging there. She went and stood beside him and watched him a few moments in her cold little way. He took no notice of her and so at last she spoke to him.

"I have been into the other gardens," she said.

"There was nothin' to prevent thee," he answered crustily.

"I went into the orchard."

"There was no dog at th' door to bite thee," he answered.

"There was no door there into the other garden," said Mary.

"What garden?" he said in a rough voice, stopping his digging for a moment. "The one on the other side of the wall," answered Mistress Mary. "There are trees there—I saw the tops of them. A bird with a red breast was sitting on one of them and he sang."

To her surprise the surly old weather-beaten face actually changed its expression. A slow smile spread over it and the gardener looked quite different. It made her think that it was curious how much nicer a person looked when he smiled. She had not thought of it before.

He turned about to the orchard side of his garden and began to whistle—a low soft whistle. She could not understand how such a surly man could make such a coaxing sound. Almost the next moment a wonderful thing happened. She heard a soft little rushing flight through the air—and it was the bird with the red breast flying to them, and he actually alighted on the big clod of earth quite near to the gardener's foot.

"Here he is," chuckled the old man.

"What kind of a bird is he?" Mary asked.

"Doesn't tha' know? He's a robin redbreast an' they're th' friendliest, curiousest birds alive. They're almost as friendly as dogs—if you know how to get on with 'em. Watch him peckin' about there an' lookin' round at us now an' again. He knows we're talkin' about him."

The robin hopped about busily pecking the soil and now and then stopped and looked at them a little. Mary thought his black dewdrop eyes gazed at her with great curiosity. It really seemed as if he were finding out all about her. The queer feeling in her heart increased. "Where did the rest of the brood fly to?" she asked.

"There's no knowin'. The old ones turn 'em out o' their nest an' make 'em fly an' they're scattered before you know it. This one was a knowin' one an' he knew he was lonely."

Mistress Mary went a step nearer to the robin and looked at him very hard. "I'm lonely," she said.

She had not known before that this was one of the things which made her feel sour and cross. She seemed to find it out when the robin looked at her and she looked at the robin.

The old gardener pushed his cap back on his bald head and stared at her a minute.

"Art tha' th' little wench from India?" he asked.

Mary nodded. "Then no wonder tha'rt lonely. Tha'lt be lonelier before tha's done," he said.

He began to dig again, driving his spade deep into the rich black garden soil while the robin hopped about very busily employed.

"What is your name?" Mary inquired.

He stood up to answer her. "Ben Weatherstaff," he answered, and then he added with a surly chuckle, "I'm lonely mysel' except when he's with me," and he jerked his thumb toward the robin. "He's th' only friend I've got."

"I have no friends at all," said Mary. "I never had. My Ayah didn't like me and I never played with anyone."

It is a Yorkshire habit to say what you think with blunt frankness, and old Ben Weatherstaff was a Yorkshire moor man.

"Tha' an' me are a good bit alike," he said. "We was wove out of th' same cloth. We're neither of us good lookin' an' we're both of us as sour as we look. We've got the same nasty tempers, both of us, I'll warrant."

This was plain speaking, and Mary Lennox had never heard the truth about herself in her life. Native servants always salaamed and submitted to you, whatever you did. She had never thought much about her looks, but she wondered if she was as unattractive as Ben Weatherstaff and she also wondered if she looked as sour as he had looked before the robin came. She actually began to wonder also if she was "nasty tempered." She felt uncomfortable.

Suddenly a clear rippling little sound broke out near her and she turned round. She was standing a few feet from a young apple-tree and the robin had flown on to one of its branches and had burst out into a scrap of a song. Ben Weatherstaff laughed outright.

"What did he do that for?" asked Mary.

"He's made up his mind to make friends with thee," replied Ben. "Dang me if he hasn't took a fancy to thee."

"To me?" said Mary, and she moved toward the little tree softly and looked up.

"Would you make friends with me?" she said to the robin just as if she was speaking to a person. "Would you?" And she did not say it either in her hard little voice or in her imperious Indian voice, but in a tone so soft and eager and coaxing that Ben Weatherstaff was as surprised as she had been when she heard him whistle.

46

Literature Comprehension

Character

A Fresh Perspective

Answer these questions about the story.

What is Mary like earlier in the story? Use as many descriptive words from the story as you can find. Include at least two of your own words to describe her.

_____

_____

What is she like at the end? Use as many descriptive words from the story as you can find. Include at least two of your own words to describe her.

_____

_____

Mary goes through a big change in the course of this story, and all that change makes her feel something. How does Mary feel after Ben makes his observations about her?

_____

_____

Why do you think this small encounter matters so much to Mary? Why does it change her so much? Include details from the story to support your ideas.

_____

_____

_____

Mary has a realization in the middle of this story. What does she realize?

_____

_____

Two things help her realize this. What are those two things?

_____

_____

Mary has her realization about halfway through this story. But she doesn't change until the end. What happens to her that causes her to change?

_____

_____

In the story, Ben tells Mary that she has made a new friend. But although the author doesn't come right out and say it, she implies that Mary has made more than one new friend. Whom does the author suggest Mary has made friends with, besides the bird?

_____

_____

Bird's-Eye View

Mary meets Ben and the robin while she's searching for a secret garden. But because the garden is locked, no one can see it except for the bird, who can fly over the wall.

Literature Comprehension

Perspective

What do you imagine you might find in a secret garden?

_____

_____

_____

_____

_____

_____

What would it feel like to be a bird that can fly?

_____

_____

_____

_____

_____

_____

Research and Analysis

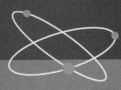

Good Question!

The first step in research is to be curious. Write down five things you wish you knew about each of the topics below.

The North Pole	Violets	The Moon

Research and Analysis

Research

Brain Box

To **research** means to gather information on a topic.

You might gather information because you're curious about a topic or you want to find out whether something is true.

The North Pole

_____

_____

_____

_____

_____

Violets

_____

_____

_____

_____

_____

The Moon

_____

_____

_____

_____

_____

A Laser Focus

Pick your favorite question from the previous page and write it here.

_____

List three other questions that would help you answer your first question.

_____

_____

_____

List five places you could look up answers to your questions.

_____   _____

_____   _____

_____

List three things you could do to find out the answer yourself.

_____

_____

_____

Brain Box

Research begins with wondering, but it doesn't stop there.

To complete your research, make a plan to find out what you want to know.

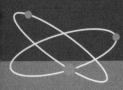

Changing the Tune

You probably have a microwave oven in your home. It wasn't invented by someone who set out to find a faster way to cook food. In fact, the first microwaves were emitted by a machine called a "magnetron." It improved the radar on Allied planes during World War II. One day, a scientist named Spencer noticed that the candy bar in his pocket melted when he stood too close to a nearby magnetron. And when he held a bag of popcorn beside the machine, the kernels popped!

What new direction would you take with your research if you found yourself in the following situations? Write at least two new ideas for each.

You've been growing cultures of a specific bacterium, hoping to run some tests on it, and you can't get enough cultures to grow. All of them seem to be dying, especially the ones in the sunlight. You're not sure why, but a bacterium you didn't mean to cultivate is now growing like crazy in your petri dishes.

_____

_____

_____

_____

You've been combing through the letters of a famous poet, hoping to learn more about her relationship with her mother. But she almost never mentions her mother. Then you discover that she had a strange habit of writing recipes on the back of her poems, and poems on the back of her recipes when she sent them to another famous poet.

_____

_____

_____

_____

Research and Analysis

Research

Brain Box

You don't always find the information that you expect to find when you embark on research. But even when you don't find the answer you were looking for, you might discover something important.

Opposites Attract

Read this letter that John Adams wrote. It describes how he and Thomas Jefferson were appointed to draft the Declaration of Independence.

Research and Analysis

Unreliable narrator

Mr. Jefferson came into Congress, in June 1775, and brought with him a reputation for literature, science, and a happy talent of composition. Writings of his were handed about, remarkable for the peculiar felicity of expression. Though a silent member in Congress, he was so prompt, frank, explicit, and decisive upon committees and in conversation, not even Samuel Adams was more so, that he soon seized upon my heart; and upon this occasion I gave him my vote, and did all in my power to procure the votes of others. I think he had one more vote than any other, and that placed him at the head of the committee. I had the next highest number, and that placed me second. The committee met, discussed the subject, and then appointed Mr. Jefferson and me to make the draught, I suppose because we were the two first on the list.

The subcommittee met. Jefferson proposed to me to make the draught. I said, "I will not."

"You should do it."

"Oh! no."

"Why will you not? You ought to do it."

"I will not."

"Why?"

"Reasons enough."

"What can be your reasons?"

"Reason first, you are a Virginian, and a Virginian ought to appear at the head of this business. Reason second, I am obnoxious, suspected, and unpopular. You are very much otherwise. Reason third, you can write ten times better than I can."

"Well," said Jefferson, "if you are decided, I will do as well as I can."

"Very well. When you have drawn it up, we will have a meeting."

List all the adjectives that John Adams uses to describe himself.

_____

List all the adjectives Adams uses to describe Thomas Jefferson.

_____

Adams describes himself as unpopular, but several facts in the letter contradict this. List at least two.

_____

At first, Jefferson refuses to draft the document, but several facts in the letter suggest he might actually want to. List at least two.

_____

_____

Brain Box

An **unreliable narrator** is a narrator who tells us things that are not supported by the facts he or she describes.

A Matter of Opinion

In the first paragraph of Adams's letter, underline everything that is a **fact**. Then circle everything that is an **opinion**.

Mr. Jefferson came into Congress, in June 1775, and brought with him a reputation for literature, science, and a happy talent of composition. Writings of his were handed about, remarkable for the peculiar felicity of expression. Though a silent member in Congress, he was so prompt, frank, explicit, and decisive upon committees and in conversation, not even Samuel Adams was more so, that he soon seized upon my heart; and upon this occasion I gave him my vote, and did all in my power to procure the votes of others. I think he had one more vote than any other, and that placed him at the head of the committee. I had the next highest number, and that placed me second. The committee met, discussed the subject, and then appointed Mr. Jefferson and me to make the draught, I suppose because we were the two first on the list.

Now write your own version of the paragraph—sticking only to the facts.

Brain Box

A **fact** is a piece of information can be proven true.

An **opinion** is a personal view on a particular thing or topic. It may or may not be based on the facts.

Star Quality

Answer the questions below about Thomas Jefferson, who is the "star" of this letter.

What is the very first thing we learn about Thomas Jefferson?

_____

What kind of reputation did Jefferson have?

_____

John Adams forms an opinion of Jefferson. What is his opinion?

_____

In Jefferson's conversation with Adams, does Jefferson live up to his reputation? Why or why not?

_____

_____

In Jefferson's conversation with Adams (see page 53), does Jefferson live up to Adams's opinion of him as "frank" and "decisive"? Why or why not?

_____

_____

What do we learn about Adams from the way he describes Jefferson? What kinds of things does Adams seem to admire? What kinds of things does he seem to be interested in?

_____

_____

_____

Brain Box

A strong argument is based on **reason**, which means it is logical and based on **evidence**.

Paraphrase or Plagiarism?

Decide whether each sentence below is **plagiarism** or **paraphrasing**.

If you think a line is too close to John Adams's original letter, paraphrase it in your own words.

In June of 1775, Thomas Jefferson joined Congress.

_____

Jefferson's writings were handed about, remarkable for the peculiar felicity of expression.

_____

In committee work, John Adams believed that nobody was more "prompt, frank, explicit, or decisive" than Thomas Jefferson—including Samuel Adams.

_____

_____

John Adams gave Jefferson his vote, and did all in his power to procure the votes of others.

_____

_____

John Adams had the next highest number, and that placed him second.

_____

After meeting, the committee appointed Adams and Jefferson to create the first draft of the Declaration of Independence.

_____

Adams told Jefferson he should write the draft because Jefferson was a Virginian, more popular than Adams, and known to be an excellent writer.

_____

_____

Brain Box

Your own ideas are often built on the ideas of others. To **plagiarize** is to present someone else's work as if it were your own. It's a form of stealing. To **paraphrase** is to restate the meaning of someone else's work in different words.

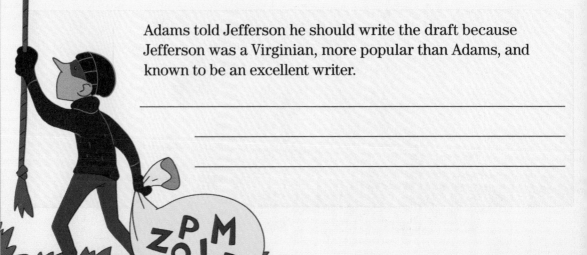

What Happened Here?

Using the sources below, conduct your own research about what happened to the missing pie.

What do you think your mom did with the pie? Quote from the evidence, and draw your own conclusions.

_____

_____

What do you think your sister did with the pie? Quote from the evidence, and draw your own conclusions.

_____

_____

What do you think the dog did with the pie? Quote from the evidence, and draw your own conclusions.

_____

_____

Which of these sources do you think is the most credible? Why?

_____

_____

Which of these sources is the least credible? Why?

_____

_____

Brain Box

Credibility means that you can believe what a source tells you.

The more credible a source is, the more you can trust it.

The less credible a source is, the more you should question it.

Our Best Guess

You might not always know what a word means.
But then you can make an **educated guess**.
What do you think the word in bold type in
each section might mean?

No matter what they did, they could never figure it out. The
answer always seemed to **elude** them.

_____

The family worked hard for years to make ends meet, but after
their father lost his job, they sank into **poverty**.

_____

She dunked the fabric into the dye, and while it was **immersed**,
she waited for it to change color.

_____

The team's training was incredibly **rigorous**: they practiced both
morning and night and didn't neglect any aspect of the game.

_____

He felt nervous until he heard her voice, which **soothed** him.

_____

The piece of music didn't seem to have any variety at all. It was so
monotonous that many of the concertgoers fell asleep.

_____

The library had a **diversity** of books, everything from ancient
history to modern astronomy and just about everything in
between.

_____

A Piece of History

Look at these pieces of **evidence** that Jon and Janine found in the basement of their historic home when they bought it. Then use the evidence to answer the questions.

New Addition

Baby Ava 1923

Certificate of Marriage
Jimmy Smith and Agnes Sparrow
in the year 1942

Baby Jimmy 1921

Mom and Dad, Florida, 1956

BABY SASHA 1922

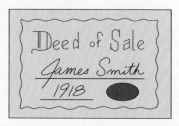

Deed of Sale
James Smith
1918

Tina and James 1919

Deed of Sale
Jimmy and Agnes Smith
1947

Who was the original owner of the house? When was it bought?

_____

When did the owner and his wife create an addition on the house?

_____

Why do you think they created the addition?

_____

Who were the next owners of the house? When did they buy it?

_____

What was the new owners' relationship to the original owners?

_____

What happened to the original owners?

_____

Brain Box

Not all information is found in books and newspapers.

Sometimes your research leads you to other kinds of sources. Gain as much information as you can from a variety of sources.

Cutting Through the Confusion

Read what Ben's older sister, Sheila, says about where she thinks the family should go for dinner. Then answer the questions below.

Research and Analysis

Persuasion

> I don't even care what we do. But I'm just saying, the last time we went to the drive-through, it was raining and my fries were soggy before I even got a single bite. I just think it's nice when a family can sit down together across a table, not all buckled into our seats. I think it's much healthier to go to a place where we can get a good salad, not just fast food. And the drive-through is always out of everything you want by the time we get there, anyway. The last time Dad ordered cheese fries, they were out of cheese. Plus, Danny Thompson is always there. Not that I care.

Do you think it's true that Sheila doesn't care where the family goes for dinner?

_____

What does she want?

_____

_____

What are her arguments against the drive-through?

_____

_____

What are her arguments for going someplace else?

_____

_____

Why do you think she really doesn't want to go to the drive-through?

_____

_____

Brain Box

Everyone has a perspective. An **argument** is the group of claims that a person makes to express a perspective. **Claims** are the facts or ideas a person offers in support of her or his argument.

Name That Source

Review the **citation guideline**. Then create citations for each of the books listed below.

Author's last name, Author's first name. <u>Title of book</u>. Place of publication: Name of publisher, Date of publication.

> Yin, Janie. <u>Pet Ducks, from Duckling to Drake</u>. San Francisco, CA: Feathered Friend Publishing, 1939.

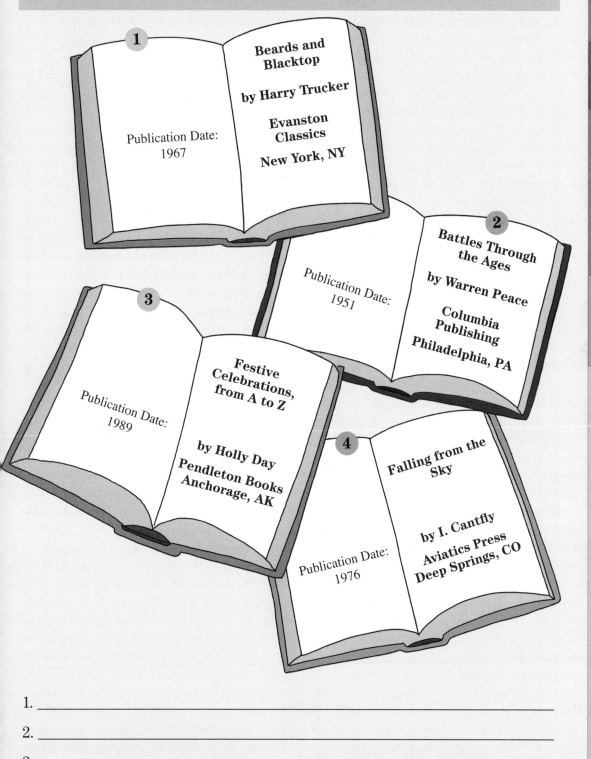

1

Beards and Blacktop

by Harry Trucker

Evanston Classics

New York, NY

Publication Date: 1967

2

Battles Through the Ages

by Warren Peace

Columbia Publishing

Philadelphia, PA

Publication Date: 1951

3

Festive Celebrations, from A to Z

by Holly Day

Pendleton Books

Anchorage, AK

Publication Date: 1989

4

Falling from the Sky

by I. Cantfly

Aviatics Press

Deep Springs, CO

Publication Date: 1976

1. _____

2. _____

3. _____

4. _____

Brain Box

A **citation** includes all the information about a source that was used in research.

Citation style may vary, so it's important to be able to arrange the relevant information about a source in any requested format.

He Said, She Said

Albert and Edwina have very different takes on the explosion in the laboratory.

Albert: Honestly, sometimes I think these beakers must get up and walk around at night when we're not here. It's either that or some of these lab assistants. They can be so careless. I feel like every time I come in, nothing is where I put it. I think somebody must have swapped the vials I usually use with something else. That's the only logical conclusion. There's simply no other possibility. I know I would never have confused them. I mean, a reaction of that kind could blow up the entire laboratory. Well, I guess we've proved that point, at least, haven't we?

Edwina: I hate to say it, but I'm afraid everyone in the laboratory has seen this coming for a long time. Albert is always misplacing things. Last week he walked out carrying one of our beakers, and left a can of soda on the Bunsen burner. Luckily, one of the lab assistants caught him before he could take a sip of the chemicals. And I pulled the can of soda off the Bunsen burner before it exploded. Almost every time I come in, I look over his things and put them back in order, to keep him out of trouble as much as I can. But I know there were several unexplained explosions at his last lab. They were never sure exactly what caused them. But I think maybe now we have our answer.

What does Albert think caused the explosion?

_____

What does Edwina think caused the explosion?

_____

From Albert's statement, how would you describe Albert?

_____

From Edwina's statement, how would you describe Edwina?

_____

Reason and Evidence

What facts or evidence does Albert use to support his claims?

_____

_____

_____

What facts or evidence does Edwina use to support her claims?

_____

_____

_____

Research and Analysis

Is Albert's claim that there is no other explanation for the explosion than a careless lab assistant reasonable? Why or why not?

_____

_____

_____

Is Edwina's claim that Albert might have had something to do with the explosion reasonable? Why or why not?

_____

_____

_____

The Big Idea

Read about what Frederick Douglass experienced when
he wanted to learn how to read. Then answer the questions.

The plan which I adopted, and the one by which I was most successful, was that of making friends of all the little white boys whom I met in the street. As many of these as I could, I converted into teachers. With their kindly aid, obtained at different times and in different places, I finally succeeded in learning to read. When I was sent on errands, I always took my book with me, and by doing one part of my errand quickly, I found time to get a lesson before my return. I used also to carry bread with me, enough of which was always in the house, and to which I was always welcome; for I was much better off in this regard than many of the poor white children in our neighborhood. This bread I used to bestow upon the hungry little urchins, who, in return, would give me that more valuable bread of knowledge. I am strongly tempted to give the names of two or three of those little boys, as a testimonial of the gratitude and affection I bear them; but prudence forbids—not that it would injure me, but it might embarrass them; for it is almost an unpardonable offence to teach slaves to read in this Christian country. It is enough to say of the dear little fellows, that they lived on Philpot Street, very near Durgin and Bailey's ship-yard. I used to talk this matter of slavery over with them. I would sometimes say to them, I wished I could be as free as they would be when they got to be men. "You will be free as soon as you are twenty-one, but I am a slave for life! Have not I as good a right to be free as you have?" These words used to trouble them; they would express for me the liveliest sympathy, and console me with the hope that something would occur by which I might be free.

I was now about twelve years old, and the thought of being a slave for life began to bear heavily upon my heart. As I read and contemplated the subject, behold! that very discontentment which Master Hugh had predicted would follow my learning to read had already come, to torment and sting my soul to unutterable anguish. As I writhed under it, I would at times feel that learning to read had been a curse rather than a blessing. It had given me a view of my wretched condition, without the remedy. It opened my eyes to the horrible pit, but to no ladder upon which to get out. In moments of agony, I envied my fellow-slaves for their stupidity. I have often wished myself a beast. I preferred the condition of the meanest reptile to my own. Anything, no matter what, to get rid of thinking! It was this everlasting thinking of my condition that tormented me. There was no getting rid of it. It was pressed upon me by every object within sight or hearing, animate or inanimate. The silver trump of freedom had roused my soul to eternal wakefulness. Freedom now appeared, to disappear no more forever. It was heard in every sound, and seen in everything. It was ever present to torment me with a sense of my wretched condition. I saw nothing without seeing it, I heard nothing without hearing it, and felt nothing without feeling it. It looked from every star, it smiled in every calm, breathed in every wind, and moved in every storm.

What is the main theme of the first paragraph?

_____

List three things Frederick Douglass does in order to learn how to read.

_____

_____

_____

At the end of the first paragraph, a new theme emerges. What is it?

_____

What is the first sentence in which the new theme is directly mentioned?

_____

Douglass doesn't mention the issue of slavery until midway through the first paragraph, but it is implied by the earlier events. How does the theme of slavery appear in the story even before Douglass uses the word?

_____

_____

_____

Brain Box

An author doesn't always come right out and say what the theme of a piece is.

Discover the theme by paying attention to the details an author chooses to give the reader.

Research and Analysis

Crucial Elements

Think about how the **themes** of reading and freedom played a major role in Frederick Douglass's life.

What is Douglass's main goal in the first part of the story?

_____

_____

What words does Douglass use to describe how he feels once he learns how to read?

_____

_____

The element of reading and the element of freedom appear in both paragraphs. What does reading have to do with freedom in the first paragraph?

_____

_____

Douglass might have expected to feel more freedom once he learned how to read. In the second paragraph, what happens instead?

_____

_____

Even as Douglass becomes frustrated with his lack of freedom, freedom takes on a larger role in the story. By the end of the story, where does Douglass see or think about freedom?

_____

_____

Brain Box

A piece of writing has a **structure**, just like a building.

That structure is composed of **elements**. But instead of wood, nails, and beams, writing is composed of **images**, **ideas**, and **themes**.

What's the Purpose?

What do you learn about Frederick Douglass from the story he tells?

What does he think about reading?

_____

_____

What does he think about the other boys he knows?

_____

_____

What words does he use to describe them?

_____

_____

What does he think about slavery?

_____

_____

What words does he use to describe his feelings about it?

_____

_____

Why do you think he chose to tell this story? What do you think he
hopes will happen when people read it?

_____

_____

_____

_____

Let Freedom Ring

Answer the questions below.

When does Frederick Douglass first introduce the idea of freedom?

_____

What images does Douglass first use to illustrate the idea of freedom?

_____

_____

What other ideas does Douglass add to elaborate on the idea of freedom? What ideas do the other boys add?

_____

_____

What images does Douglass use to illustrate the idea of freedom in the second paragraph?

_____

_____

What idea is implied by the way Douglass illustrates freedom?

_____

_____

_____

Research and Analysis

Analysis

Brain Box

A new idea is introduced the first time you read about it.

It is **illustrated** with examples and **elaborated** by more details that develop ideas.

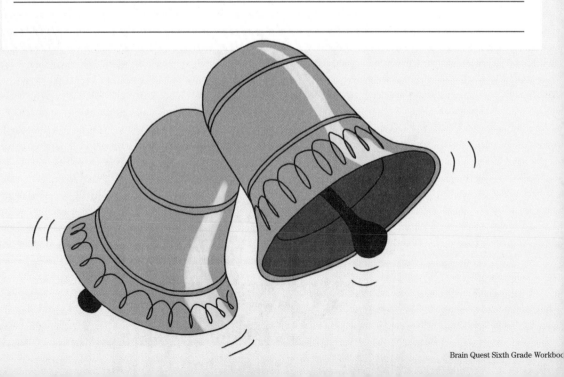

Translation, Please!

Translate the **jargon** below into simpler words that anyone could understand.

"Your honor, my client has sworn to her version of the facts in this **affidavit**."

_____

_____

"If you're having any problems with your ears, nose, and throat, you'll need to see an **otolaryngologist**."

_____

_____

"When your computer needs a temporary spot to store information, it'll **cache** it."

_____

_____

"We poured a slab of concrete under the wall to create this **footing**, and there's another one that helps support that column."

_____

_____

"If there's not very much of that liquid left, you can store it in the **microcentrifuge**."

_____

_____

Brain Box

Jargon is language that is mainly used in a specific field, like medicine, law, or engineering. Jargon can be hard to understand at first, but often you can figure out the meaning by context clues.

That's Your Opinion

Read this student's research paper. Underline all the facts and circle all the opinions. Highlight the **conclusion**.

Everybody knows ducks are the best animals in the world. The scientific name for the duck family is *Anatidae*. It's a beautiful name. Female ducks are called "hens" or "ducks." Male ducks are called "drakes." And baby ducks are called "ducklings." There isn't anything cuter in the world than a duckling. And speaking of the world, there are ducks all over the world—except for Antarctica. Their webbed feet would probably get pretty cold on all that snow, because they don't have any fur to cover them. The ducks are covered with down, which mother ducks use to create a soft nest for their children. Ducks aren't fussy eaters, either. They're omnivores, which means they eat everything from grass to insects to fruit and fish. Ducks were domesticated as farm animals and pets over 500 years ago. All the domestic ducks in the world are descended from two kinds of ducks: either a mallard or a Muscovy. But today, there are many more domestic breeds of ducks—over 40. Ducks have always been my favorite kind of animal, and I hope now they're yours, too.

Write your own version, with only the facts. Put the facts in the order you think makes the most sense.

Research

If you were researching this topic, what other questions would you like to explore?

_____

Brain Box

A **conclusion** is a final judgment or reasoned opinion. Authors often use facts and logic to lead to their conclusion.

Writing

Making Sense

Imagine you're going to a carnival. Now imagine that you're missing one of your senses when you go.

What would it be like to visit the carnival if you couldn't see? What kinds of things would you hear, touch, smell, and taste? What would you think about them?

_____

_____

_____

_____

Writing

If you had to give up one sense, which sense would you give up?

_____

Description

What would you miss the most about that sense?

_____

If you could only keep one sense, which sense would you keep?

_____

Why is that sense so important to you?

_____

_____

_____

_____

Write a story about everything you'd like to do when you visit the carnival. Describe the things you'd see and do. Make sure you also include at least one sentence about what you would see, smell, taste, touch, and hear.

Writing

Description

Brain Box

Whenever you describe something, give people a sense of what it looks or sounds like and how it feels, tastes, and smells.

That helps other people feel as if they were really there, too.

Watch Your Tone!

You talk to your friends differently from how you talk to your teachers. Rewrite the statements below as if you were talking to a teacher rather than a friend.

"Give me that!"
_____

"I hate this exercise. It's stupid."
_____

"I don't get this. What's going on?"
_____

"Are we ever going to be done with this?"
_____

"Here, you can have this."
_____

"This is awesome!"
_____

Writing

Tone

Brain Box

Tone isn't what you say; it's the way you say it.

You change your tone depending on your **audience** (who your readers are).

It's important to use the right tone for the audience.

Otherwise, people might not listen to what you have to say.

A Formal Affair

It's good to use **formal language** when it's appropriate. But it's not appropriate all the time. Sometimes **informal language** is better. Ask yourself: What is the best way to say this?

Rewrite the statements below as if you were talking to a friend.

"I must say, I'm enjoying this quite a bit."

_____

"Would you be so good as to hand me the butter?"

_____

"Would you care to join me on a walk down to the store?"

_____

"I think I'd like to go now, if that's all right with you."

_____

"I'm not sure I understand what you're saying."

_____

"Thank you very much. I appreciate it."

_____

Writing

Formal and informal tone

Brain Box

Formal language is language you use in official or professional situations to show your respect for the people around you.

Informal language is language you use in personal situations to show that you are comfortable with the people around you.

Steady On

This essay has a confusing mix of **formal** and **informal** tones. Underline all the informal language you can find. Circle any examples of formal language.

Many people believe that Socrates was the greatest philosopher who ever lived. In fact, some consider him to be the father of all philosophy. Philosophy is about the meaning of life and that kind of stuff. Socrates lived in Greece, in the fifth century BCE. I guess people kind of studied philosophy before him, but he really made it into a big deal. Philosophy used to be just for eggheads who wanted to sit around and talk about ideas. But Socrates had a different way of teaching. He didn't tell his students what to think. Instead, he asked them questions about what they thought, and helped them arrive at the answers themselves. Socrates was also interested in the practical implications of philosophy: how it applied to regular people in day-to-day life. And that interest in the consequences of philosophy may have been Socrates's downfall. Eventually, he got himself killed by talking too much about what philosophy had to do with politics. But he had the last laugh. Because they couldn't kill his ideas. So everybody still has to read him today, two thousand five hundred years later.

Writing

Formal and informal tone

Brain Box

Once you understand your audience and establish a proper tone, it's important to be **consistent**: to keep the same tone throughout a piece of writing.

Now rewrite the paragraph, maintaining a **formal tone** in all the places where you noted informal language.

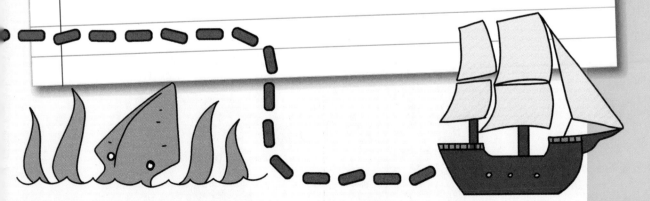

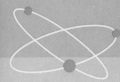

Nice to Meet You

Introducing a topic is a lot like introducing a person. You want to be sure you transmit basic facts, like who the person is. However, you also want to capture the readers' interest and give them a reason to care.

State your opinion on each of the topics below, with a sentence or two that clearly states what you think. Try to make the reader want to know more.

Curfews

_____

_____

Homework

_____

_____

College

_____

_____

Summer Vacation

_____

_____

Writing

Introductions

Brain Box

The first step in any piece of writing is to **introduce** your topic.

No matter how good your argument or evidence, people can't understand what you're thinking about if you don't clearly introduce your claim: tell them exactly what your perspective is.

Let's Talk

You speak differently from the way you write.

Imagine you are at a football game when a strange object appears over the field. As the crowd watches in fascination, the object lands on the 30-yard line, and a gang of strange blue creatures pours out and delivers extraterrestrial ice cream to every member of the crowd.

Then imagine how you would tell that story to one of your good friends.

Writing

Dialogue

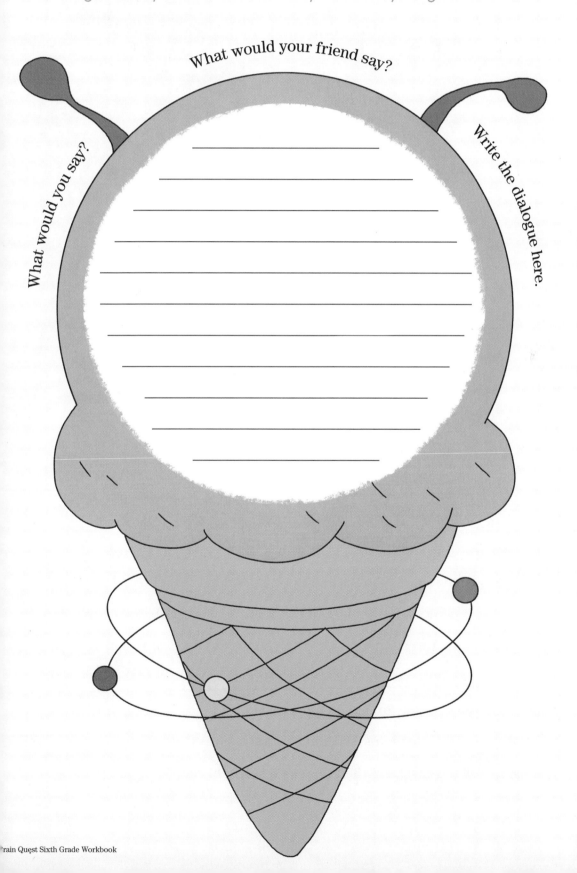

What would your friend say?

What would you say?

Write the dialogue here.

Brain Box

Dialogue is writing that reports direct speech: what people actually say in conversation.

Moving On

You give people signals when you're about to make a turn in a car or on a bike. Likewise, you need to give your readers signals when you make a turn in your writing. To do that, you use **transitional words or phrases**.

However

On the other hand

In conclusion

Furthermore

For example

Writing

Transitions

Complete the sentences in the paragraph by using the transitional words and phrases above.

Many people think summer is the best time of the year. _____,

I've always been fond of winter. In other words, I'm a fan of frigid weather.

_____, I don't particularly like being hot. Therefore, the sunshine

and high temperatures other people enjoy in the summer don't appeal to me.

_____, I try to spend most of my time indoors during the heat of the

day, when other people are out soaking up sun. _____, my favorite

part of summer is the nights, when the temperatures drop. _____,

I'm happier in a snowstorm than I am on a sandy beach.

And Then What?

When you do something is often just as important as *what* you do. Fill in the blanks in this recipe, using the **transitional words or phrases** below.

Next	Meanwhile
First	Finally

Writing

Transition

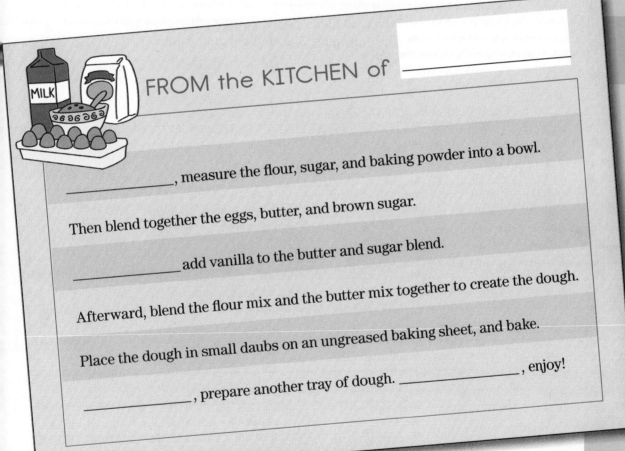

FROM the KITCHEN of _____

_____, measure the flour, sugar, and baking powder into a bowl.

Then blend together the eggs, butter, and brown sugar.

_____ add vanilla to the butter and sugar blend.

Afterward, blend the flour mix and the butter mix together to create the dough.

Place the dough in small daubs on an ungreased baking sheet, and bake.

_____, prepare another tray of dough. _____, enjoy!

Brain Box

A **transition** is the moment when you move from one idea to the next. If you don't signal to readers when you make a transition, it can be hard for them to follow your ideas.

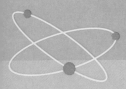

The Spice of Life

Most of us would get pretty bored if we had to eat the same thing every day for lunch. The same thing is true when we read sentences, it's no fun to read the same sentence structure over and over. Instead, vary the way you express things, so that the reader stays interested.

Rewrite the paragraph below by adding as much variation as possible to the sentence structure.

There are a lot of different kinds of orchids. There are 25,000 orchid species. Some scientists think there might be even more we haven't discovered yet. Orchids are part of the *Orchidaceae* family. Orchids look like insects. Orchids look like the kinds of insects they try to attract. Orchids also look like humans. Orchids almost seem to have faces, some people think. Orchids have been around for a long time. Scientists found ancient orchid pollen on a bee encased in amber. The pollen was millions of years old. Some orchids are actually a spice. The vanilla plant is an orchid.

Writing

Sentence variety

Brain Box

You can vary your sentences by alternating short and long sentences, using different sentence openers, and combining two sentences with a conjunction and proper punctuation.

First Impressions

When you meet a new character in a story, it's just like meeting a person in real life: **First impressions** matter. So make sure you give characters a thorough introduction when they first appear.

Using the facts below, write a few sentences to introduce each character.

NAME: Angela Parker

APPEARANCE: curly brown hair, brown eyes, athletic build

CHARACTER: stubborn but generous

PROFESSION: dog walker

LIKES/DISLIKES: likes good music/dislikes cats

_____

_____

Writing

NAME: Barney Judge

APPEARANCE: blond hair, slightly balding, blue eyes, tall

CHARACTER: shy and creative

PROFESSION: artist

LIKES/DISLIKES: likes maple syrup/dislikes crowds

_____

_____

Character characteristics

Now introduce the following character as the narrator. Instead of using "he" or "she," use "I."

NAME: Ishmael Melville

_____

APPEARANCE: unkempt hair, crooked teeth, striped shirt

_____

CHARACTER: observant and determined

_____

PROFESSION: sailor

_____

LIKES/DISLIKES: likes the open sea/dislikes white whales

_____

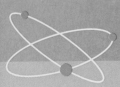

Pace Yourself

The writer of the story below spends a lot of time concentrating on unimportant details—and not much time describing the most interesting parts. Rewrite the story, using better **pacing** to improve the story's flow.

Writing

Pacing

> The race started out with a big bang. There were thousands of people at the starting line. They were wearing all kinds of crazy costumes, because it was the annual Turkey Trot. Some of the runners wore standard running gear, like athletic shoes, warm-up pants, tights, or moisture-wicking shirts. Some of them wore hats with turkey gobbler decorations. One man had a big sheaf of fake feathers pinned to his back. There was even a woman who had brought a live turkey on a leash. The pace of the race wasn't very fast, but the turkey did create a bit of drama at the end of the race. Two runners had been neck and neck the whole time, but at the very end, the turkey escaped. It "goosed" one of the runners—and she sprang forward at the last minute and won the race.

Brain Box

Pacing refers to how quickly a story unfolds.

When you write a story, you don't want to spend too much time on things that don't matter, or too little time on things that do matter.

Building a Case

Why should you get to run the school for a day?

Write sentences that contain each of the following elements to support your argument:

Fact: _____

Description: _____

Quotation: _____

Example: _____

Reason: _____

Writing

Elements

Brain Box

Facts are pieces of information that can be proven true.

Description gives details about the way something is.

Now write your campaign speech using the information and evidence you gathered on the previous page.

Brain Box

A **quotation** is something somebody else said or wrote.

An **example** illustrates a point.

A **reason** is a statement that supports an argument.

High Definition

Before you tell somebody your opinion about something, you need to **define** what it is.

Write a sentence that describes each of the items below. Make your definitions as complete as possible.

MY DEFINITION

Mountain

_____

_____

Bird

_____

_____

Cloud

_____

_____

Airplane

_____

_____

Skydiver

_____

_____

Using a dictionary, look up the definition of each word. Write down any words or phrases that were not included in your definition.

THE DICTIONARY

Mountain

_____
_____

Bird

_____
_____

Cloud

_____
_____

Airplane

_____
_____

Skydiver

_____
_____

Were your definitions different from the dictionary definitions? How?

_____
_____

Would you make any changes to your definition after reading the dictionary definition?

_____
_____

Brain Box

A **definition** expresses the meaning of a word or a phrase.

90

Chickens and Eggs

The **cause** of an event will help you understand *why* things happen. Then you can guess *what* might happen next—the **effect**. Imagine each of the events below. Then write another sentence or two about what might happen next.

Cause: The first thing everybody in the neighborhood heard each morning was the old rooster's crow.

Effect: _____

_____

Cause: The plump brown hen laid two eggs that day, instead of one.

Effect: _____

_____

Cause: None of the chickens would come out of the coop, no matter how much the farmer's wife coaxed them.

Effect: _____

_____

Cause: The price of feathers for stuffing down pillows doubled that year.

Effect: _____

_____

Cause: One day, all of Farmer Grant's hens suddenly began to lay blue eggs instead of white eggs.

Effect: _____

_____

Writing

Cause and effect

Brain Box

Why did something happen? That's the **cause**.

What happened? That's the **effect**.

Eggs and Chickens

Next, imagine that all the sentences you just read weren't the cause. Instead, they're the effect.

This time, write a sentence or two imagining what must have come first.

Cause: _____

_____

Effect: The first thing everybody in the neighborhood heard each morning was the old rooster's crow.

Cause: _____

_____

Effect: The plump brown hen laid two eggs that day, instead of one.

Cause: _____

_____

Effect: None of the chickens would come out of the coop, no matter how much the farmer's wife coaxed them.

Cause: _____

_____

Effect: The price of feathers for stuffing down pillows doubled that year.

Cause: _____

_____

Effect: One day, all Farmer Grant's hens suddenly began to lay blue eggs instead of white eggs.

Ready for Class

Which of these objects would you take with you to each of the classes listed below?

English: _____

_____

Physical Education: _____

_____

Science: _____

_____

Write a few sentences about which of the objects you would take with you to each class, and why.

_____
_____
_____
_____
_____

Are there any objects that you might take with you to more than one class? Why?

_____
_____
_____
_____

Writing

Classification

Brain Box

To **classify** is to sort things.

You look at how things are different or similar in order to group them.

Compare and Contrast

List three things that science and physical education have in common. List three ways that science class is different from physical education.

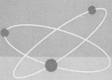

SIMILARITIES

Science:

_____

_____

_____

Physical Education:

_____

_____

_____

DIFFERENCES

Science:

_____

_____

_____

Physical Education:

_____

_____

_____

Now write a short paragraph to compare and contrast science class with physical education. Use your list of similarities and differences to write the paragraph.

_____

_____

_____

_____

_____

_____

_____

_____

Writing

Compare and contrast

Brain Box

When you **compare** things, you notice how the things are similar and different.

When you **contrast** things, you focus on the way they differ.

In Conclusion

Read each of the paragraphs below. At the end of each paragraph, write a sentence that draws a logical conclusion.

Writing

Drawing
conclusions

The whole town pitched in for the benefit dinner for the family who had lost everything in a fire. The soccer team cooked piles of spaghetti. The fire department baked hundreds of meatballs. The garden society used all the tomatoes it had grown that season in a savory sauce.

_____

_____

_____

When is the right time to plant a new seedling? If you plant too early in the spring, it might be frozen by a late frost. If you plant too late in the summer, it may not have enough time to flower or bear fruit before the season ends.

_____

_____

_____

There were only three people in the house at the time the jewelry was stolen. One of them spent the entire time waving to friends from a first-floor window. One of them was a baby who hadn't yet learned how to walk.

_____

_____

_____

Order! Order!

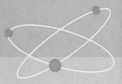

Number the events below in **chronological order**.

| | The witness box exploded in a shower of white sparks and blue smoke. |

| | As the guilty magician took the stand, he fastened a wad of exploding gum to his chair in the witness box. |

| | But when the court finally came to order again, the magician had vanished. |

| | The whole court erupted into chaos. |

| | When the questioning became uncomfortable, the magician struck a match to the exploding gum. |

| | The judge pounded her gavel and called for order. |

Writing

Chronological order

Now write a paragraph that introduces the events, tells the story, and draws a conclusion.

Show and Tell

What's the story here? Take a close look at these graphs. Then write a paragraph that explains the story they tell.

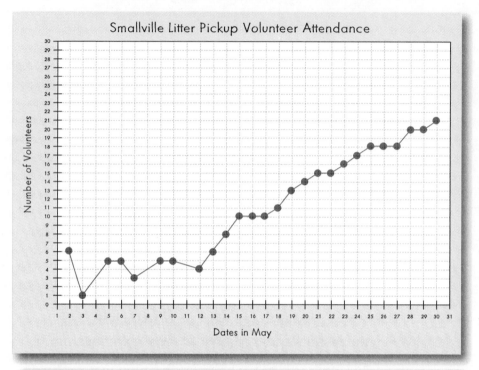

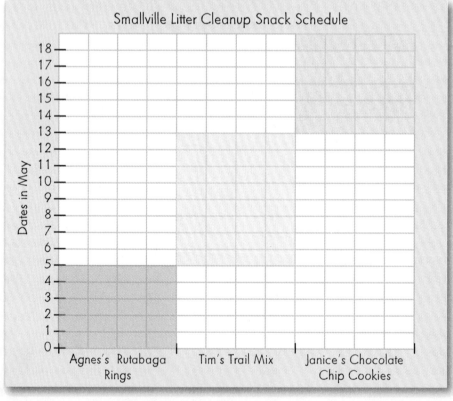

_____

_____

_____

_____

_____

Planning Ahead

Imagine you are writing a report on the city of Paris. Brainstorm five questions about Paris that you want to answer for your readers.

For each question, note where you might do research to find the answer.

Then think about the order in which the questions would fit best in your report, and number them 1 to 5.

Writing

Brainstorming

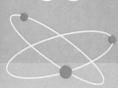

A New Perspective

Sometimes when you research an idea or revise your writing, you discover that your ideas have changed.

Read Cara's argument for why she should be allowed to go to the amusement park. Then rewrite it, using the same evidence, to argue that she should stay home this time.

Writing

Revising

There's no reason why I shouldn't be allowed to go to the amusement park again this year. I know Mrs. Collins was all worried when she couldn't find me for six hours last year, but I was fine that whole time. I did let go of my Cherry Freeze on the first big turn of the Iron Raptor, but I think the dress I was wearing looks even cuter in pink than it did when it was all white. And it didn't hit *that* many people when it landed on the crowd below. Only about a dozen people, out of the hundreds who were standing there. Some of them were even wearing white, so it's like I started my own pink trend. And I guess I did get kind of jostled around because I didn't wear my seat belt after I snuck onto the log ride. My arm kind of hurt on the way home, but I was feeling so queasy from all the popcorn and cotton candy I ate that I barely noticed. It didn't take the doctor very long to put the cast on my broken arm, and six weeks later, I was as good as new. I had a great time, and I can't wait to go again!

Writing

Revising

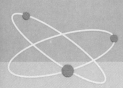

First Draft

Read this first draft. It is full of good ideas, but also full of errors. Circle every error you find.

every year, the NAB (National Basketball Association) in June holds a draft too add new members to the league. International and U.S. college players. College players who have already played four years of college football are automatically eligible for the draft. Others have to declare their eligibility. Drafts have two rounds. A lottery determines which teams get to pick first. Then different teams pick the players they think will play best. In the end, only 60 Players total are selected, out of the entir country. They're the newest members of the NBA.

Then rewrite the draft correcting the errors and adding your own personal style.

Writing

Revising

Brain Box

In writing, a **draft** is just another way of saying "version."

Your first **draft** is your first try at writing your ideas down.

Every time you make changes to a piece of your writing, you create a new draft.

Pronouns and Punctuation

On the Case

Detectives solve cases. Did you know languages have **cases**, too?

Read about each detective case below. Then circle the appropriate pronoun to replace the italicized nouns.

Subjective

Sherlock was a great detective and the subject of many stories.

(He/Him/His)

Sherlock and Doctor Watson worked together to solve cases.

(They/Them/Their)

Objective

No matter the mystery, Sherlock solved every one of *his cases*.

(they/them/theirs)

Sherlock was fascinated with *a mysterious woman named Irene*.

(she/her/hers)

Possessive

Sherlock's great mind was his prized possession.

(He/Him/His)

Sherlock depended on Doctor Watson as a partner but even more on *his and Doctor Watson's* friendship.

(they/them/their)

Brain Box

Cases tell you if the pronoun that is replacing the noun should be **subjective**, **objective**, or **possessive**. The pronoun needs to be in the same case as the word it replaces.

A pronoun should be in the **subjective case** if it replaces the subject of a sentence, which is the source of the action.

A pronoun should be in the **objective case** if it replaces the object of a sentence, which has something happening to it.

A pronoun should be in the **possessive case** if the pronoun must indicate that something belongs to someone.

In Which Case?

Sort these pronouns into the proper case.

he	they	her
them	his	him
our	us	their
her	she	we

If you need a hint, try inserting each pronoun into these sample sentences. When you find a fit, you've found its case!

NOTES

Subjective:

_____

_____

_____

_____ solved the case.

NOTES

Objective:

_____

_____

_____

The case almost stumped _____.

NOTES

Possessive:

_____

_____

_____

It was _____ case.

Bonus question: Is there any pronoun that is in more than one case? If so, which one or ones?

_____

The Correct Case

Detective Parker's report has the facts straight, but the cases are all wrong—at least as far as his pronouns are concerned. Circle each incorrect pronoun, and write the proper pronoun above it.

Me arrived on the scene just after 10:30 p.m. The entire family was standing in the yard. Mr. Smith reported that him saw a strange shadow in the living room. Bobby, the son, claimed his heard weird noises sometime before its dad. Him reported its to Mrs. Smith, whom told he to go back to bed. Me investigation led I to the living room, where my followed the noises and discovered Pete, the family dog. Him was curled up beside a lamp that had fallen from a nearby table. As me approached, my saw another small furry object near the lightbulb: A tiny kitten Pete was keeping warm. Me carried its outside and introduced the newest member to the rest of the family.

Pronoun, Please!

Pronouns are used to add variety to sentences. Without them, each time you mention a person, you would have to use a full name—like the writer of this letter. Mark each place where a pronoun can be used instead of a noun. Then write the pronoun you can use to replace the noun.

I'm having a great time here at camp. I'm learning how to ride a

horse this week. My favorite horse is a mare named Sparkplug.

Sparkplug is the fastest horse in the stables. Sparkplug can't run

for as long as the other horses, but Sparkplug can beat them all

in a short race. Sparkplug can also jump like a champ. Sparkplug

is fast, but Sparkplug is gentle. Sparkplug is actually very patient

with me. Even though Sparkplug can run faster than any of the

other horses, when Sparkplug knows Sparkplug has a new rider

on Sparkplug's back, Sparkplug won't try to go too fast. But I'm

getting comfortable enough now that I can trot and even canter

without feeling too scared. And one day soon I'll get to take

Sparkplug out and actually feel what it's like when Sparkplug

gallops. I can't wait!

Brain Box

A **pronoun** is a word that takes the place of a noun.

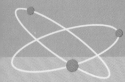

That's Intense

Complete each sentence with an **intensive pronoun**.

herself	myself
itself	yourself
ourselves	himself
yourselves	themselves

He picked the colors out _____ .

All of you saw it _____ with your own eyes.

I, _____ , never really liked that song.

We can figure that out _____ .

I'm afraid you're going to have to do that _____ .

The monster's face _____ scared them even
more than the spooky music.

She found that old box of cables and
then carried it home _____ .

When she discovered the mess
they made, she told them
they'd have to clean it up _____ .

Pronouns and Punctuation

Intensive pronouns

Brain Box

Intensive pronouns help add emphasis to the subject of a sentence.

Often, intensive pronouns immediately follow the subject, but not always.

Disappearing Act

Circle the **intensive** or **reflexive pronoun** in each sentence below.

Then omit the reflexive or intensive pronoun when you read the sentence. If the sentence still makes sense, check the box for intensive. If it doesn't make sense, check the box for reflexive.

intensive   reflexive

☐ ☐ He'd learned how to rely on himself.

☐ ☐ I always liked her myself.

☐ ☐ Please, talk among yourselves.

☐ ☐ She wanted to be sure that he didn't just love her for her money, but for herself.

☐ ☐ When they couldn't get someone to help them, they went ahead and did it themselves.

☐ ☐ Speak for yourself!

☐ ☐ We'd really like to see that for ourselves.

☐ ☐ She herself didn't really like root beer, although she always served plenty of it at parties.

Pronouns and Punctuation

Reflexive pronouns

Brain Box

Reflexive pronouns refer to a subject mentioned earlier.

The same words are used for both **intensive** and **reflexive** pronouns, words such as **myself**, **yourself**, and **ourselves**.

So how can you tell if it's an intensive or a reflexive pronoun? By taking the word out!

You, Yourself

Write a sentence for each of the following topics using the pronoun provided as a reflective or intensive pronoun.

balloon, myself:

_____

_____

tigers, themselves:

_____

_____

_____

basketball, herself:

_____

_____

_____

fireworks, ourselves:

_____

_____

mountain, himself:

_____

_____

party, yourselves:

_____

_____

_____

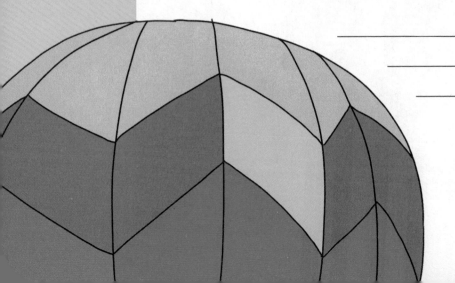

It's Personal

Read the sentences below. Then rewrite them with the pronoun indicated.

We rushed down the stairs, but the train pulled away before we reached the platform.

Second person: **you**

_____

_____

You have a beautiful voice, and it's a pleasure to hear.

First person: **I**

_____

_____

I wished it hadn't rained today, so that the game hadn't been canceled.

Third person: **she**

_____

_____

He was delighted to discover a candy bar at the bottom of the bag when he finished unpacking the groceries.

Third person: **they**

_____

_____

She discovered a new path in the woods and followed it until she found a hidden stream.

First person: **we**

_____

_____

Pronouns and Punctuation

Pronouns

Brain Box

First person means you are talking about yourself, using words like **I** or **we**.

Second person means you are talking directly to someone else, using words like **you** and **yours**.

Third person means you are talking about someone else, using words like **he**, **she**, and **they**.

Brain Quest Sixth Grade Workbook

Anything and Everything

Circle the verb that correctly completes each sentence of this story.

Everybody agrees/agree.

Somebody were/was in the classroom after school let out.

Everything have/has been moved around.

Anyone knows/know that the empty fish tank doesn't belong on the teacher's desk.

And someone has/have filled it with fresh-picked strawberries.

Nobody is/are sure who did it.

But no one really minds/mind much.

Everyone are/is too busy enjoying the treat.

Brain Box

An **indefinite pronoun** is one that refers to an unspecified person, thing, or amount.

Shifting Gears

Circle the pronoun in each sentence that doesn't agree
with the person in the sentence. Then write the proper pronoun.

When we went to the zoo, you had to pay extra to see
the dolphin exhibit. _____

When my dad was my age, you could see more stars because there was
less light pollution. _____

I like to go down to the river because you can watch the ships go by.
_____

If you enjoy reading, they should be able to find a book at the library.
_____

When we get to the museum, you have to be very polite to the guards.
_____

After you add the sugar, then we add the cinnamon. _____

We discovered you could go in through a special side entrance to the
botanical gardens. _____

Brain Box

When you change a pronoun without changing the noun it represents, it is like adding a new person to the sentence (or causing one to disappear) without warning.

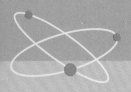

Got Your Number

Circle the word that correctly completes each sentence with the proper **pronoun number**.

If Bobby comes by and tries to sell us another box of cookies, tell them / him we don't want one.

If the customer has a special coupon, they / she is entitled to buy two azaleas for the price of one.

Janet and Candace went downtown to pick up their / her band uniforms.

The whole class helped Jasper look for his / their harmonica.

A dancer must put in many hours to develop her / their technique.

The boy's whole basketball team worked hard to make sure he / they were in shape.

When the deliveryman arrives, please have them / him leave the package on the porch.

Pronouns and Punctuation

Pronoun number

Brain Box

Pronoun number indicates whether a pronoun refers to a singular noun or a plural one. If the pronoun refers only to one person, the pronoun should be singular. If the pronoun refers to more than one person, the pronoun should be plural.

Whoops!

Pronouns refer to a noun that was mentioned earlier. So when we use a pronoun that doesn't refer to anything else, it can be very confusing.

All the sentences below contain pronouns that don't refer to anything. Circle the pronoun that's missing its antecedent.

They tell me the weather is great in Florida this time of year.

In my school, they let us out just before three o'clock.

They always say the best offense is a good defense.

In shop class, you learn to work with metal.

The coach did not like the way the referee called it.

In my family, they use a lot of delicious spices.

After graduation, you will have all kinds of opportunities to consider.

Brain Box

The word or noun that a pronoun replaces is called its **antecedent**.

View from Above

This student has a great story to tell, but he or she doesn't understand how pronouns work. Underline every pronoun that has an unclear antecedent or doesn't have an antecedent at all.

They say there's nothing like a bird's-eye view. But you have a hard time getting a bird's-eye view if you don't have wings—unless you go up in a hot-air balloon like I did last weekend. My dad and brother were with me, and he loved it! Everywhere you looked, it was a beautiful view. We saw an airplane. And a bird landed right on the edge of the balloon's basket. When we came down, they even let us wave to some of the people in the fields below. I just wanted to stay until the next time the balloon went back up, but my dad said we had to go. But as my dad helped my brother out of the basket, he said it wouldn't be the last time we got to go for a balloon ride.

Now rewrite the story from the previous page, so that every pronoun has a clear antecedent.

By the Way

Read the pairs of sentences below. Then write a checkmark next to the sentence that contains a **nonrestrictive**, or **parenthetical**, **element**.

Are you stumped? Try taking the element out. If the sentence still makes sense, the element is parenthetical!

☐ a. Sarah Harper, the captain of the girls' basketball team, was also a science whiz.

☐ b. Science whiz Sarah Harper was also the captain of the girls' basketball team.

☐ a. In fall, when school opens, students flood back into classrooms.

☐ b. Students return to school in the fall.

☐ a. The team in blue quickly defeated the team in white.

☐ b. The visiting team, dressed in blue uniforms, won a quick victory.

☐ a. If you'd come home when I asked—instead of stopping to buy candy—we wouldn't have missed the bus.

☐ b. We wouldn't have missed the bus if you hadn't stopped to buy candy, but had come home when I asked.

☐ a. Many students enjoy visiting the beach during the summer months and skating on the lake in winter.

☐ b. Many students enjoy visiting the beach, which is very beautiful.

Pronouns and Punctuation

Nonrestrictive/
parenthetical
elements

Brain Box

Nonrestrictive elements, also called **parenthetical,** are clauses that are not essential to the meaning of a sentence.

They tell us something that's nice to know, but if we take it out, the sentence will still make sense.

Make Your Choice

Identify the nonrestrictive, or parenthetical, element in each sentence. Then choose a type of punctuation to set it off: parentheses, commas, or an em dash. On the line underneath each sentence, explain why you chose that punctuation. There isn't always a "right" answer about which punctuation to use. But it's important to know why you chose that punctuation.

Every autumn we love to scare ourselves silly at the haunted house.

_____

_____

It seemed like a lot of money to him almost five hundred dollars, so he was delighted when he received the check.

_____

_____

Isaac M. Singer, who invented the modern sewing machine, also designed boats.

_____

_____

Nobody liked to stay after school especially on days when the football team was playing so everyone was on their best behavior.

_____

_____

_____

Jennifer Bates who planted the community garden took baskets of fresh vegetables around to all of the neighbors.

_____

_____

_____

Pronouns and Punctuation

Nonrestrictive/
parenthetical
elements

Brain Box

There are three kinds of punctuation to set off nonrestrictive (parenthetical) elements.

Parentheses indicate that the element isn't very important to the major topic.

Commas indicate that the element is a part of the general discussion.

Em dashes show that you want to emphasize the element.

The Case of the Missing Pronouns

Many of the pronouns in this story are missing. Fill in the blanks by using clues from the surrounding sentences. Remember to use the correct number and case.

The whole Parker family had just piled into the family car when _____ realized that something was missing. Riley, the family dog, wasn't in his usual place in the very back of the van. _____ couldn't go to the lake without _____ . So _____ all got out of the car to look for _____ . Susie got on _____ hands and knees to check under the porch, where Riley liked to dig. Susie's mom checked the cozy pile of clean laundry _____ had just folded, where Riley often liked to nap. Susie's dad walked up and down the block and called for Riley to come to _____ . And Susie's brother, Jimmy, ran upstairs to _____ room, where Riley spent most nights guarding _____ bed. Finally, _____ all gave up and returned to the car. There was Riley, right where _____ belonged, on _____ dog seat in the back of the van, just as if _____ had been waiting for _____ all along.

Pronoun Police!

This story contains all sorts of pronoun errors. Can you spot them all?
Circle every incorrectly used pronoun you find.

> Officer Cornbloom was convinced there was a robber
> in the neighborhood. Him and his partner always heard
> sounds coming from the abandoned lot. When he got
> there, you could see the place was empty. The sounds
> never stopped, until he arrived on the spot. It was a real
> mystery to he and his partner, and it almost drove they
> crazy. Then, in the spring, they finally cracked the case.
> All over the abandoned lot, beautiful flowers sprang up.
> And the rascally kids who had been planting at night came
> out and admitted to they're "crimes."

Then rewrite the story to eliminate all the errors you found.

Clear That Up

A vague **antecedent** can be just as confusing as a missing antecedent.
Rewrite each of the following sentences to make it clear.

As Jen was telling Ann the story, she laughed.

_____

_____

The golfer ran the golf cart into the snack stand, but it was not damaged.

_____

_____

The clown apologized to the lion tamer, but he was still angry.

_____

_____

As April steered Ginger on the toboggan to the bottom of the hill,
she started to scream.

_____

_____

Every time my dad goes to visit my grandfather,
he is happy.

_____

_____

Metaphor and Meaning

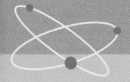

A Touch of Class

Read these groups of words that have **Greek or Latin affixes**.
Then write your best guess about what the affix means.

Brain Box

An **affix** is a part of a word that appears at the beginning or end of the root. It can add to a word's meaning or change it completely.

Many English words have Greek or Latin affixes.

audible, auditorium, audiovisual

_____

biology, anthropology, geology

_____

semiannual, semicircle, semisweet

_____

decade, December, decagon

_____

artist, dentist, pianist

_____

benevolent, benediction, beneficial

_____

submarine, submerge, subbasement

_____

Our Classical Roots

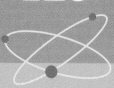

Read these groups of words that have **Greek or Latin roots**.

Then match each group to the definition that best defines the original Greek or Latin word.

DEFINITIONS

philosopher, sophisticated, sophomore	remember
donate, donor, pardon	light
enamored, amiable, amorous	love
astronomy, asteroid, asterisk	give
bibliography, bibliomania, Bible	star
memento, commemorate, memorable	book
luminous, translucent, lunar	wise

Brain Box

A **root** is a word or part of a word that can tell the word's basic meaning.

You can make better guesses about what English words mean when you begin to recognize Greek and Latin roots.

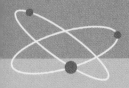

Getting to the Root

For each of the pairs of words below, underline the Greek or Latin **root** or **affix**. Then think of another English word that has the same Greek or Latin root or affix. Make your best guess about what the original Greek or Latin root or affix might mean.

	third word	**meaning of root or affix**
spectacle, spectator	_____	_____
anniversary, biannual	_____	_____
symmetry, sympathy	_____	_____
automobile, automatic	_____	_____
telegram, telescope	_____	_____
conform, formation	_____	_____
admire, mirror	_____	_____
antonym, pseudonym	_____	_____

Metaphor and Meaning

Roots and affixes

Bonus: Use an online resource of Greek and Latin roots to check.

The Proper Case

Are these pronouns **subjective**, **objective**, or **possessive**?
Put each one into its proper "case."

they	hers	I
me	we	theirs
ours	them	her
him	he	us
mine	yours	she

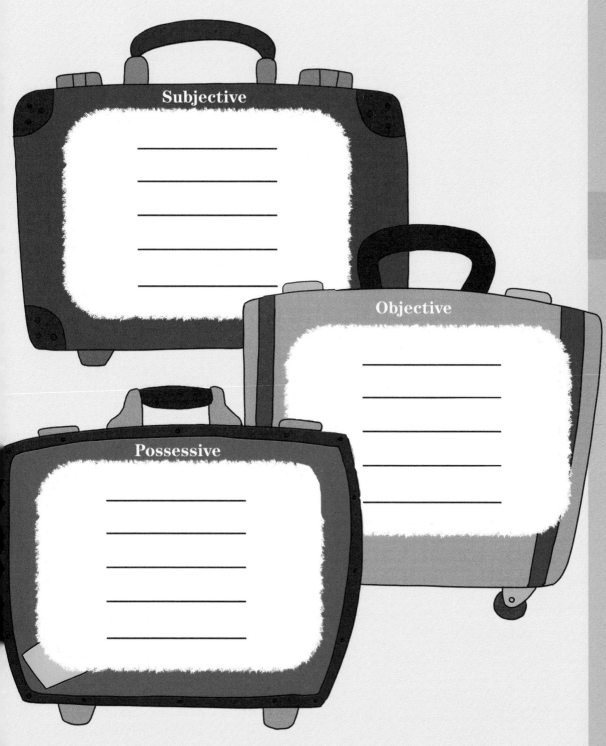

Subjective

_____
_____
_____
_____

Objective

_____
_____
_____
_____

Possessive

_____
_____
_____
_____

Metaphor and Meaning

Subjective, objective, and possessive case

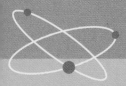

Look It Up!

Look up the words below in a print or online dictionary. Then write the definition next to each word.

accommodate: _____

_____

_____

predicament: _____

_____

_____

boisterous: _____

_____

_____

resolute: _____

_____

_____

ingenious: _____

_____

_____

subordinate: _____

_____

_____

unanimous: _____

_____

_____

Look up the words below. When you find each, sound it out using the pronunciation guide. Then write down the part of speech for each word.

monotonous

_____

deteriorate

_____

conspicuous

_____

priority

_____

anticipate

_____

exaggerate

_____

omniscient

_____

ə..........**b**anana, c**o**llide, **a**but
ã..........**day**, f**a**de, d**a**te, **a**orta, dr**a**pe, c**a**pe
ä..........b**o**ther, c**o**t
ē..........**ea**sy, m**ea**ly
ī..........s**i**te, s**i**de, b**uy**, tr**i**pe
ȯr..........b**oar**, p**or**t, d**oor**, sh**or**e
sh..........as in **sh**y, mi**ss**ion, ma**ch**ine, spe**ci**al (actually this is a single
            sound, not two); with a hyphen between two sounds as in
            grasshopper \ˈgras-, hä-pər\
ü ....**ru**le, y**ou**th, **u**nion, \yün-yən\, f**ew** \ˈfyü\

Metaphor and Meaning

Pronunciation

Brain Box

A dictionary doesn't just give the meaning of a word.

It also gives a word's **pronunciation**, which shows how to say the word aloud.

And it gives a word's **part of speech**, such as noun, pronoun, verb, adverb, adjective, conjunction, article, or preposition.

A Second Opinion

Look up the definition to each of the words below in a print or an online dictionary. Write your own definition for each word. Then write anything you notice about how those definitions might be different.

agony
_____
_____

preliminary
_____
_____

reinforce
_____
_____

improvise
_____
_____

diversity
_____
_____

Get a Clue

Read each sentence below. Based on the way the boldfaced word is used in the sentence, write your own definition for that word.

The waters outside the harbor were so full of sharp rocks that they weren't just dangerous to passing ships, but downright **treacherous**.

_____

The judge deliberated until he came to a conclusion about the case, and then he returned to the courtroom and announced his **verdict**.

_____

Alice tried to keep her **composure** when she met her favorite author, but she was so excited that it was almost impossible for her to stay calm.

_____

On the observation deck at the top of the skyscraper, Alex accidentally let go of his lollipop, and it **plummeted** to the sidewalk far below.

_____

The wild pears were so **abundant** that they filled up both the buckets Jack had brought to hold them, and his hat as well.

_____

Now look each word up in a dictionary. Is the dictionary definition different from your context guess? If so, how?

_____

_____

_____

Metaphor and Meaning

Context clues

Brain Box

Most of the time, you learn what a word means and how it should be used by hearing someone else use it or by reading it in **context**.

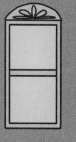
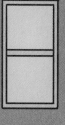
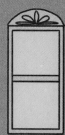
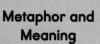

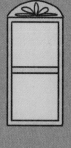
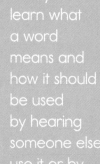
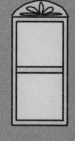

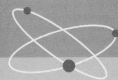

Define Yourself

Now it's your turn. Make up five new words. Write your own definition for each below. And don't forget to note the part of speech for each new word!

word: _____

part of speech:_____

definition: _____

_____

word:_____

part of speech: _____

definition: _____

_____

word: _____

part of speech: _____

definition: _____

_____

word: _____

part of speech: _____

definition: _____

_____

word: _____

part of speech: _____

definition: _____

_____

Give Us a Clue

How would a person use your new words? Write a sentence or two using each of your new words. Make sure anyone who reads the sentences will understand what your new words mean and how to use them.

_____

_____

_____

_____

_____

_____

_____

_____

Metaphor and Meaning

Definitions

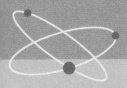

Literally!

Each sentence below contains **figurative language**. But what is the writer actually trying to say? Translate the figurative language into **literal language**.

The sky was weeping.

That wrestler was a bear.

You're my sunshine.

It was a dark day.

This tastes like heaven.

She's a hurricane.

The old door complained as it swung open.

Metaphor and Meaning

Literal and figurative language

Brain Box

Literal language is an exact or direct way of expressing something.

Figurative language uses more expansive or imaginative meanings of words. Some kinds of figurative terms or phrases are called **figures of speech**.

I Like That

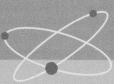

Complete each sentence below with your own figure of speech without using adjectives. To write a **simile** or a **metaphor**, compare each thing to something else. For example: "A friendship is a treasure."

Simile

A day off school is like . . .

_____

Missing a friend is like . . .

_____

A slice of warm apple pie is like . . .

_____

Metaphor

A good teacher is . . .

_____

A loud voice is . . .

_____

A long walk is . . .

_____

Brain Box

A **simile** compares essentially unlike things using "like" or "as."

A **metaphor** is a figure of speech in which one thing is used as a symbol for something else.

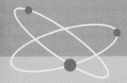
How Do You Feel?

How would objects feel if they had feelings? What would they think if they had thoughts?

Write a few sentences describing the thoughts or feelings of each of the objects in the phrases below.

Metaphor and Meaning

Personification

A bike left out in the rain

_____

_____

A bouquet of flowers carried by the winner of a contest

_____

_____

A jacket forgotten in the gym

_____

_____

The last piece of a cake

_____

_____

A favorite pair of shoes

_____

_____

Brain Box

Personification is a kind of figurative language that imagines that objects have thoughts or feelings just like a person.

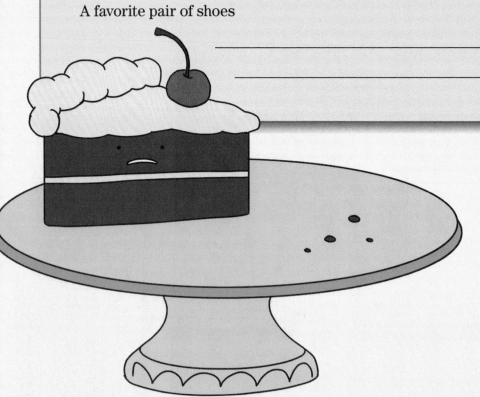

Cause and Effect

What can you learn about the boldface word from the effect it has on the action in the sentence?

Write as many facts as you can.

When the **economy** began to improve, interest rates went down, wages rose, and prices in stores even dropped slightly.

_____

_____

The man claimed he had invented eyeglasses that could see into the future, but eventually the eyeglasses were revealed to be a **hoax**, so the scientists who had vouched for them were disgraced.

_____

_____

For centuries, the city was known as a **sanctuary**, so people who had committed crimes or run afoul of powerful leaders would flee there to find safety.

_____

_____

Metaphor and Meaning

Context clues

The big man didn't mean to **intimidate** the kids, but they were so afraid of his hulking size that when they first met him, they ran and hid.

_____

_____

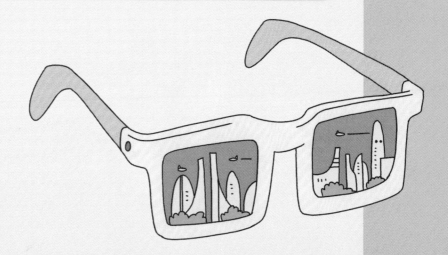

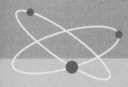

Piece of Cake!

How much can you learn about one word from another word in the same sentence?

Answer the questions below to find out.

A **quart** of milk is 32 ounces, and there are usually 8 **ounces** in a glass.

How many glasses of milk are there in a quart?

_____

About what amount is one ounce?

_____

In the **quarry**, big machines peeled back the dirt to mine for valuable **shale**.

What is a quarry?

_____

What is shale?

_____

Alaska is the largest **state** of the fifty states in the **nation**.

Is a state or the nation bigger?

_____

What is the nation made of?

_____

Metaphor and Meaning

Context clues

Brain Box

Some words describe things that are **part of a whole.**

When you recognize this, you can often learn something about the part from the whole and about the whole from the part.

Category Clues

Based on the clues in each sentence below, fill in the blank with the proper item, or category.

| tomatoes | clouds | ferns |
| tree frog | lighthouse |

The gladiator _____ is found mostly in Costa Rica, Panama, Colombia, and Ecuador, and spends its life in trees, like all other members of its species.

With its beautiful white brick facade and powerful beam, the Storm Point _____ is one of the most beautiful examples of its kind on the entire coast.

Thin, wispy cirrus, which appear high in the sky, and fluffy cumulus, which appear lower to the ground, are two of the most common types of _____ .

Metaphor and Meaning

Context clues

Chefs prize the rich flavor of the Roma for sauces, and home cooks enjoy the compact pop and bright color of the cherry or grape varieties, all of which are among the most popular varieties of _____ .

Brain Box

A **category** is a group of things that are like each other. Once you know something is part of a category, you know it is like other things in that category.

And you also know that other things in that category are alike.

The bold, showy fronds of the cinnamon and the shy curl of the fiddlehead both have their place among the _____ of the forest.

What's in a Word?

Match the words below with their **associations** or **connotations**.

happy

content

glad

cheerful

jolly

delirious

thrilled

madness

Santa Claus

roller coaster

cheerleader

birthday

to meet you

satisfied

Metaphor and Meaning

Associations and connotations

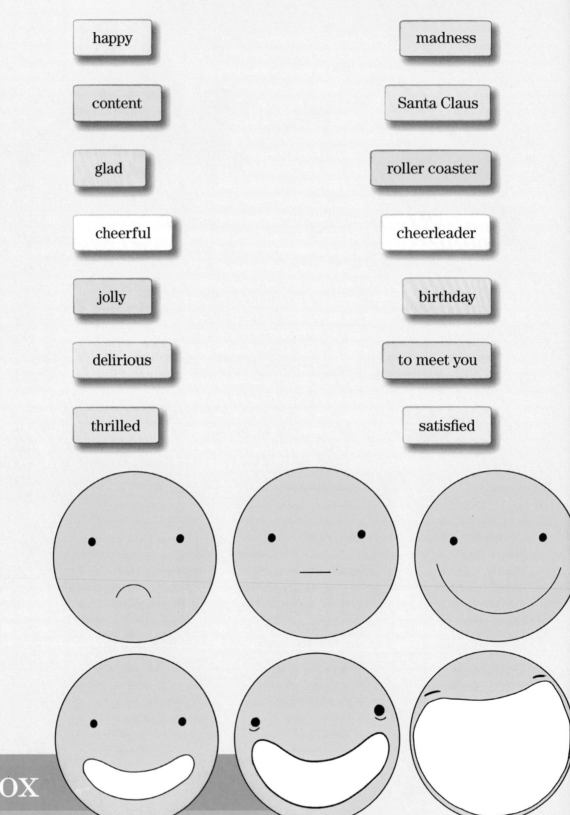

Brain Box

Some words mean similar things.

Some words may have more than one **connotation**, or a feeling or an idea that the words give along with their main meaning.

Other words may have different **associations**, or other contexts in which you're also used to seeing or hearing the word.

Close But Not Quite!

Write one sentence for each of the words below. In your sentences, show how the words in each pair differ.

rest   relax

_____

_____

thoughtful   brooding

_____

_____

play   recreation

_____

_____

Metaphor and Meaning

Shades of meaning

hope   expect

_____

_____

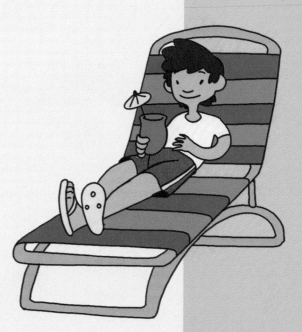

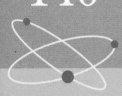

The Best Fit

Circle the word that best fits in each sentence below.

The president's opinion on the new law was a source of great
| controversy | bickering | .

The two scientists | colluded | collaborated | on the
groundbreaking paper.

When they saw the enemy encampments, they knew they had
wandered into | hostile | nasty | territory.

The student was | jumpy | apprehensive | about the results
of the test, but when they came back, he was overjoyed.

Metaphor and Meaning

Shades of meaning

Her mother used to sing her lullabies to | soothe | appease | her
when she felt sick.

He just seemed to have a | knack | dexterity | for fixing cars.

The captain of the team remained | resolute | stubborn | ,
despite the fact that they were down several points.

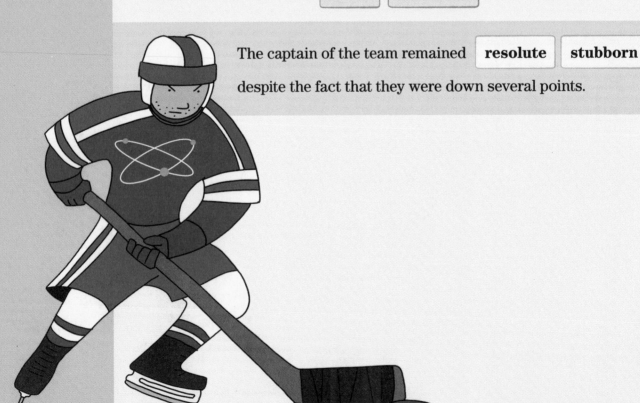

You Exaggerate

This student has a flair for **hyperbole**.
Underline the **figurative language** in this story.

As soon as I got home, my mother dropped the bomb. No sports for me until my chores were done, even though everybody in the world was already over at the park, playing without me. I was a prisoner in my own home. And let me tell you, she really cracked the whip. I worked like a dog. It took me forever, but I finally finished. Then I raced like a maniac over to the park, just in time to take the last at bat. But what an at bat! The ball went right over the fence and into the Fishers' backyard. I had literally knocked it out of the park.

Then translate the figurative language into literal language.

_____

_____

_____

_____

_____

_____

_____

_____

_____

_____

Metaphor and Meaning

Hyperbole

Brain Box

Hyperbole is a form of figurative language that uses exaggerated statements to catch the listener's attention and add emphasis.

A Bit of Color

This engineer had an exciting day, but her report is pretty dry.
Rewrite the report. Use **similes**, **metaphors**, and even **hyperbole**
to help the reader get a better feel for what happened.

We began our test of the new B-63 Human Flight Device at dawn.
I served as the first test subject and was carefully strapped into
the device, with my arms fastened to the wings and my torso and
legs fastened to the frame. On liftoff, it immediately became clear
that we had misjudged the strength of the boosters. I ascended
about three times as fast as we intended, and was unable to avoid
making contact with a low-flying flock of starlings. My height briefly
allowed me an excellent view of the surrounding countryside,
which included hilly farms dotted with livestock, such as sheep
and peacocks. However, the miscalculation with the boosters also
affected my fuel consumption, so my fuel ran out before I could
observe more, and my attention turned to the problem of landing
without power. Luckily, our failsafe technology operated perfectly.
I extended the coasting wings and glided safely to earth.

Metaphor and Meaning

Figurative language

Math
Skills

Stars in the Sky

Find the number of stars in the sky.

$$256 \times 781$$

$$193 \times 479$$

$$821 \times 534$$

$$386 \times 695$$

$$603 \times 190$$

$$777 \times 934$$

Math Skills

Multiplication

$$414 \times 282$$

$$518 \times 873$$

$$950 \times 322$$

$$279 \times 116$$

$$211 \times 408$$

$$224 \times 410$$

Brain Box

In math, the **product** is the answer we get when we multiply two or more numbers.

How Many Berries?

To find the total number of berries each customer bought, multiply the number of boxes they bought by the number of berries in each box.

$$\begin{array}{r} 22 \\ \times\ 150 \\ \hline \end{array}$$

$$\begin{array}{r} 38 \\ \times\ 934 \\ \hline \end{array}$$

$$\begin{array}{r} 61 \\ \times\ 578 \\ \hline \end{array}$$

$$\begin{array}{r} 12 \\ \times\ 256 \\ \hline \end{array}$$

$$\begin{array}{r} 56 \\ \times\ 716 \\ \hline \end{array}$$

$$\begin{array}{r} 29 \\ \times\ 393 \\ \hline \end{array}$$

$$\begin{array}{r} 45 \\ \times\ 321 \\ \hline \end{array}$$

$$\begin{array}{r} 73 \\ \times\ 452 \\ \hline \end{array}$$

$$\begin{array}{r} 15 \\ \times\ 846 \\ \hline \end{array}$$

Math Skills

Multiplication

$$\begin{array}{r} 80 \\ \times\ 821 \\ \hline \end{array}$$

Making Weight

Multiply to find how much weight a truck has to bear when it carries each big slab of rock.

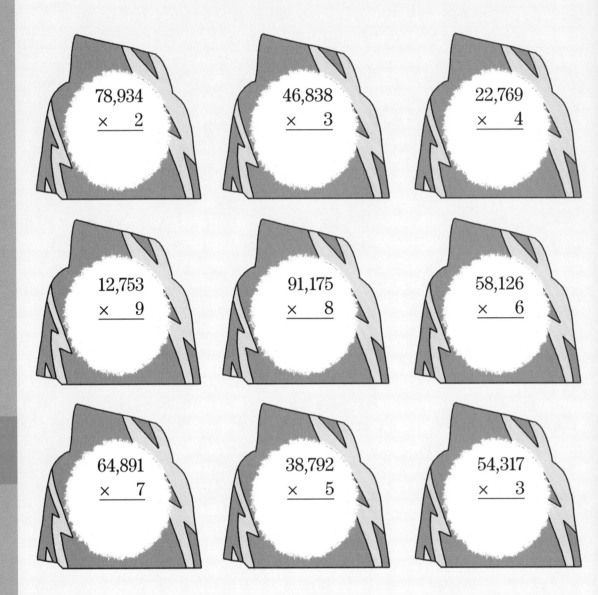

$$78,934 \times 2$$

$$46,838 \times 3$$

$$22,769 \times 4$$

$$12,753 \times 9$$

$$91,175 \times 8$$

$$58,126 \times 6$$

$$64,891 \times 7$$

$$38,792 \times 5$$

$$54,317 \times 3$$

Math Skills

Multiplication

Cutting Cable

Divide to find how long the pieces are when you cut a long cable into pieces. Show your work.

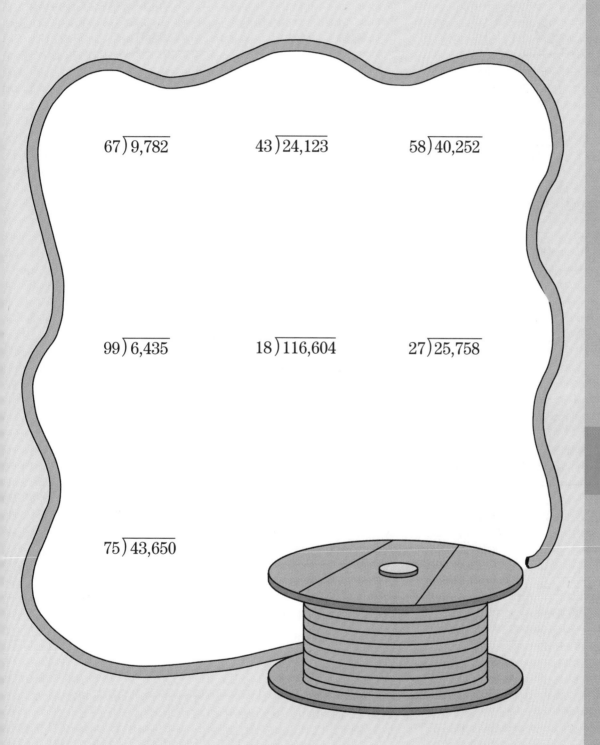

$67\overline{)9{,}782}$ $43\overline{)24{,}123}$ $58\overline{)40{,}252}$

$99\overline{)6{,}435}$ $18\overline{)116{,}604}$ $27\overline{)25{,}758}$

$75\overline{)43{,}650}$

Dividing Plunder

Each ship has a different number of pirates on board, and they must split up their booty. Divide to find how many coins each pirate gets.

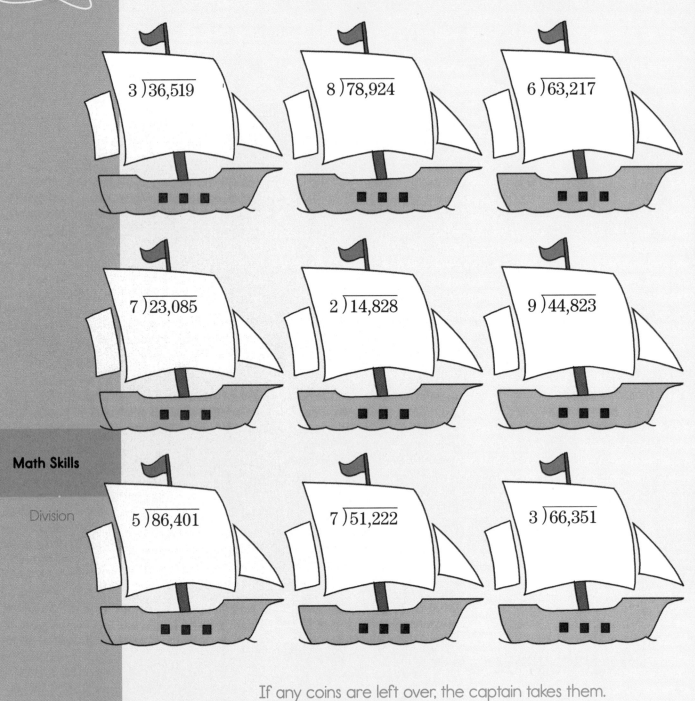

$3 \overline{)36{,}519}$

$8 \overline{)78{,}924}$

$6 \overline{)63{,}217}$

$7 \overline{)23{,}085}$

$2 \overline{)14{,}828}$

$9 \overline{)44{,}823}$

Math Skills

Division

$5 \overline{)86{,}401}$

$7 \overline{)51{,}222}$

$3 \overline{)66{,}351}$

If any coins are left over, the captain takes them. Circle any remainders above, then add them up to figure out the captain's share.

Measure Twice, Cut Once!

Divide. Then check your answer by multiplying.

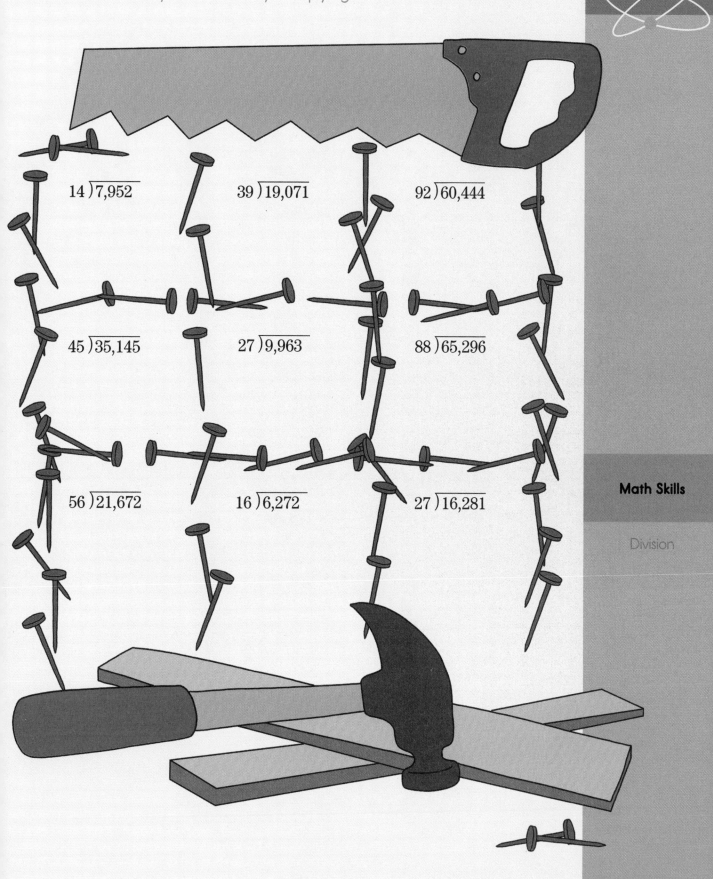

$14\overline{)7,952}$

$39\overline{)19,071}$

$92\overline{)60,444}$

$45\overline{)35,145}$

$27\overline{)9,963}$

$88\overline{)65,296}$

$56\overline{)21,672}$

$16\overline{)6,272}$

$27\overline{)16,281}$

Math Skills

Division

What's Missing?

Multiply or divide to find the missing number.

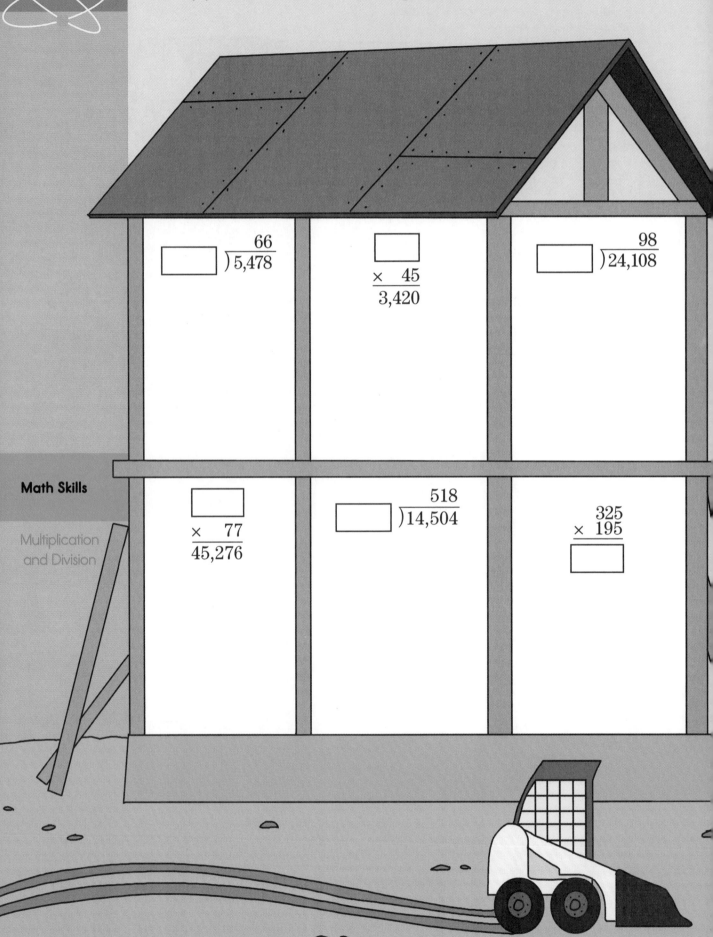

$$\boxed{}\overline{)\,5{,}478}^{\,66}$$

$$\begin{array}{r}\boxed{}\\ \times\quad 45\\ \hline 3{,}420\end{array}$$

$$\boxed{}\overline{)\,24{,}108}^{\,98}$$

$$\begin{array}{r}\boxed{}\\ \times\quad 77\\ \hline 45{,}276\end{array}$$

$$\boxed{}\overline{)\,14{,}504}^{\,518}$$

$$\begin{array}{r}325\\ \times\ 195\\ \hline \boxed{}\end{array}$$

Ratios and Proportions

Sports Night

Fill in the blanks.

The ratio of pair of cleats to studs
is _____ : _____,
because for every _____ pair of cleats,
there are _____ studs.

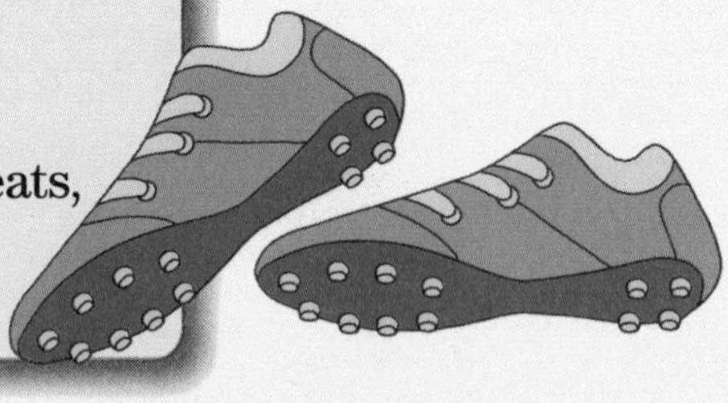

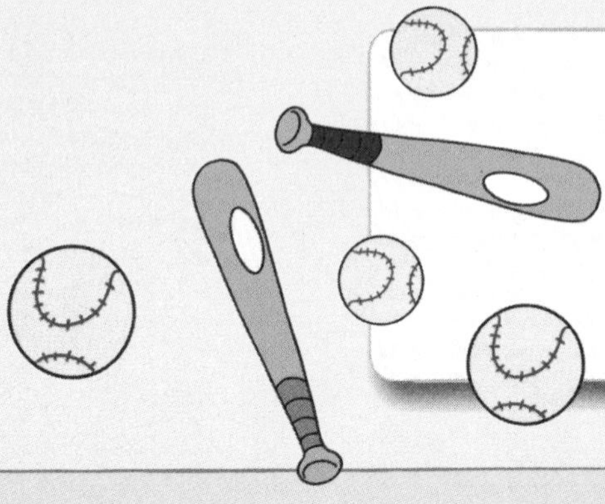

The ratio of bats to balls
is _____ : _____,
because for every _____ bats,
there are _____ balls.

The ratio of blue players to red players
is _____ : _____,
because for every _____ blue players,
there are _____ red players.

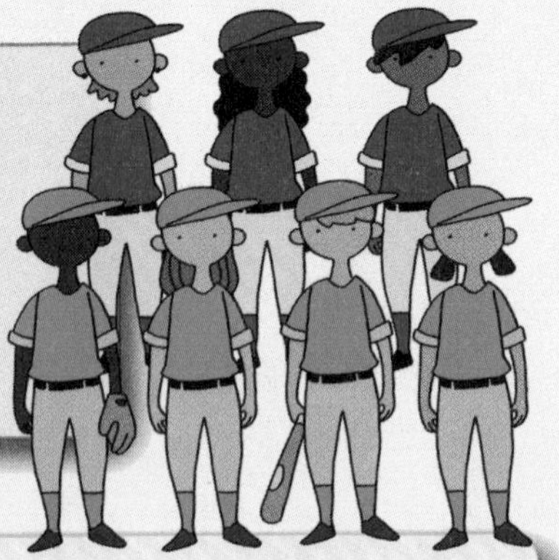

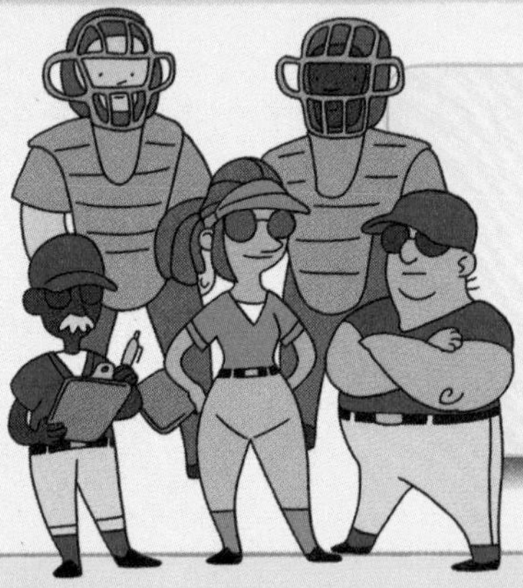

The ratio of umpires to coaches
is _____ : _____,
because for every _____ umpires,
there are _____ coaches.

The ratio of blue team points to red team points
is _____ : _____, because for every _____
points the blue team has, the red team has _____
points.

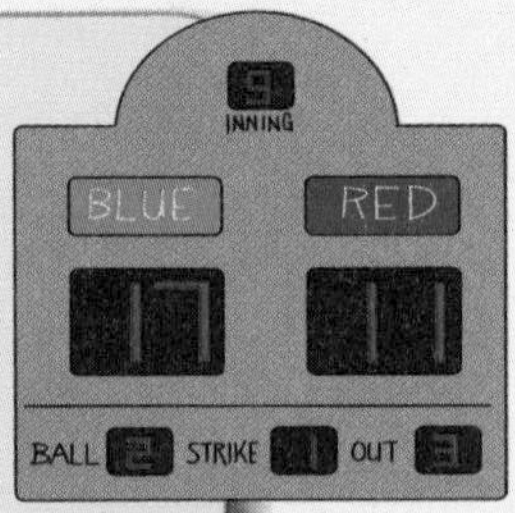

Pet Parade

Fill in the blanks.

It took the parade 1 hour to travel 17 blocks, which is a rate of _____ blocks per _____.

Mrs. Walton sold bags that each contained 5 of her homemade dog treats, which is a rate of 5 _____ per _____.

Jerry's pet rooster crowed 34 times over 17 blocks, which is a rate of _____ crows per _____.

The 3 Richardson kids brought their 9 new kittens, which is a rate of _____ kittens per _____.

Four kittens managed to escape from their wagon every 2 blocks, which is a rate of _____ escapes per _____.

Brain Box

A **rate** is a special kind of ratio that compares measurements of different units. In a rate, there is always just 1 of the second unit—for example, 32 ounces per gallon or 55 beats per minute.

How Much Is That?

Calculate the price of each grocery item.

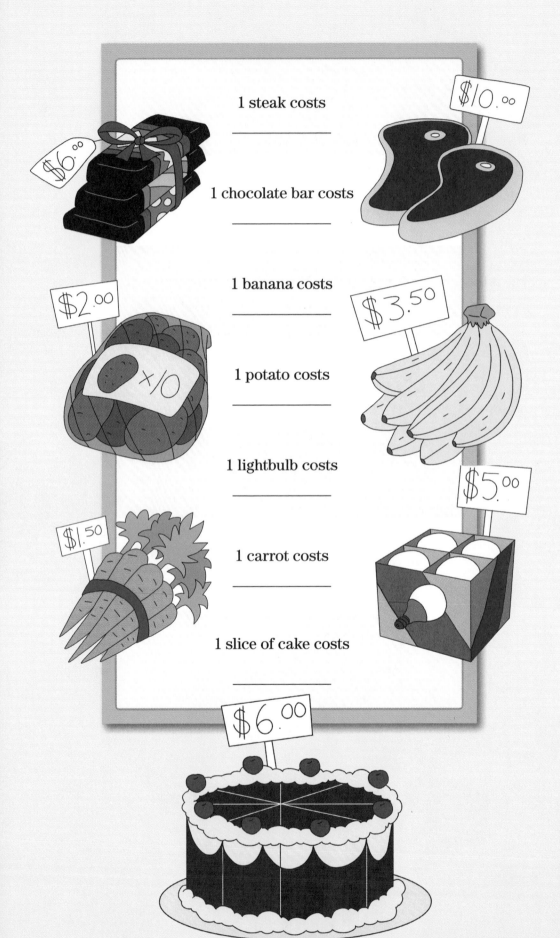

1 steak costs

_____

1 chocolate bar costs

_____

1 banana costs

_____

1 potato costs

_____

1 lightbulb costs

_____

1 carrot costs

_____

1 slice of cake costs

_____

$6.00

$10.00

$2.00

$3.50

$5.00

$1.50

×10

$6.00

Are We There Yet?

Fill in the blanks with the unit rate.

Mom drove the 180 miles from home to the hotel in 3 hours. How many miles did she drive per hour? _____

Tim swam 15 laps of the hotel pool in half an hour. How many laps could he have swum per hour? _____

Janice climbed up 1,000 feet of rocky cliff in 2 hours. How many feet did she climb per hour? _____

Dad ran 5 miles in 45 minutes. How many minutes per mile did he run? _____

The whole family hiked the 6 miles to the canyon floor in 3 hours. How many miles per hour did they walk? _____

Ratios and
Proportions

Ratios

Egg Race

Farmer Grant's chickens only ever lay 1 egg each. Farmer Johnson's chickens always lay 2 eggs. Complete each table by filling in the missing numbers.

Farmer Grant

Number of Chickens	Number of Eggs
1	1
☐	2
☐	4
☐	8
10	10
15	15
50	50

Farmer Johnson

Number of Chickens	Number of Eggs
1	2
2	4
4	☐
8	16
☐	20
15	☐
☐	100

Transformers

Express each ratio as a fraction and each fraction as a ratio.

$\frac{3}{4}$

_____

$\frac{4}{16}$

_____

19:20

_____

$\frac{5}{8}$

_____

7:10

_____

$\frac{10}{16}$

_____

Bonus: Are any of the 6 problems equivalent? If so, which ones?

_____

_____

Brain Box

Ratios can be expressed as fractions, and fractions can be expressed as ratios.

That's Not Fair!

Help Ben figure out if his brother has been fairly sharing the bag of jellybeans they bought. Circle the pairs of equivalent ratios.

Brain Box

How do you tell if two ratios are **proportional** or equivalent?

First, express both ratios as fractions.

Then multiply the numerator of each fraction by the denominator of the other.

If your answer is the same for both, then the ratios are equivalent. For example, the ratios 1:2 and 5:10 are equivalent as shown here:

$$\frac{1}{2} \diagdown\!\!\!\!\diagup \frac{5}{10}$$

10 = 10

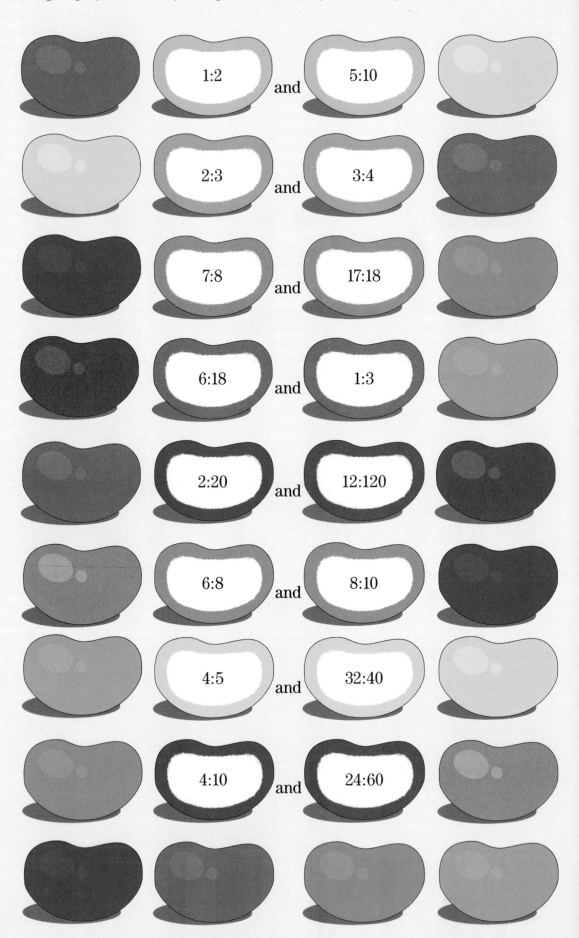

1:2 and 5:10

2:3 and 3:4

7:8 and 17:18

6:18 and 1:3

2:20 and 12:120

6:8 and 8:10

4:5 and 32:40

4:10 and 24:60

Percent Participation

Answer the questions.

The marching band has 100 members. Twelve of them play the flute. What percentage of the band members play the flute?

The basketball team has 50 members, and 18 of them are 6th graders. What percentage of the team is in the 6th grade?

The principal sent a message to 25 students to ask them to help pick up litter after school. Only 8 of them showed up. What percentage of the students came to pick up litter?

The chess club offered free ice pops to 200 students. Only 170 students accepted the treat. What percentage of the students who were offered an ice pop took one?

Thursday afternoon, 80 kids visited the library. Of those students, 60 checked out a book before they left. What percentage of the students who visited the library checked out a book?

Ratios and Proportions

Percentages

Brain Box

A **percentage** expresses a part of 100.

A Day in the Park

Solve these percentage problems.

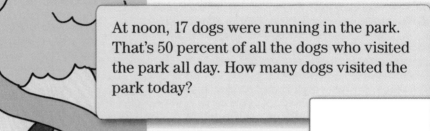

At noon, 17 dogs were running in the park. That's 50 percent of all the dogs who visited the park all day. How many dogs visited the park today?

The west entrance to the park is guarded by 3 lion statues. That's 20 percent of all the statues in the park. How many statues are in the park?

The sycamore grove contains 30 sycamore trees. That's 75 percent of all the sycamore trees in the park. How many sycamore trees are in the park?

Ratios and Proportions

Percentages

Four hundred tulips grow in the tulip field. That's 80 percent of all the tulips in the park. How many tulips are in the park?

In the oak forest, 60 kids are playing capture the flag. That's 40 percent of all the kids in the park. How many kids are in the park?

A New Perspective

Complete each diagram by filling in the correct number of boxes.

The math teacher assigns 2 pages of homework each night.
The social studies teacher assigns 5 times as many pages.

MATH

SOCIAL STUDIES

1 BOX = 1 PAGE

The home team hit 4 home runs.
The visiting team hit 2.5 times that amount.

HOME TEAM

VISITING

1 BOX = 1 HOME RUN

The news per staff spent 3 days writing the article.
The printer took 21 days to print the issue.

TIME TO WRITE

TIME TO PRINT

1 BOX = 3 DAYS

**Ratios and
Proportions**

Ratios

The concert choir raised $1,000 to go on tour.
The glee club raised one–fifth that of amount.

CONCERT CHOIR

GLEE CLUB

1 BOX = $200

Details in the Diagram

Use the double line diagram to answer each question.

How many miles will Julia have run in 45 minutes?

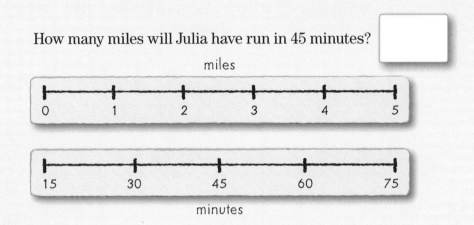

miles

| 0 | 1 | 2 | 3 | 4 | 5 |

| 15 | 30 | 45 | 60 | 75 |

minutes

How many pages will Oscar have read in a week?

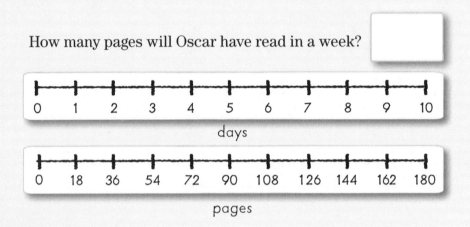

| 0 | 1 | 2 | 3 | 4 | 5 | 6 | 7 | 8 | 9 | 10 |

days

| 0 | 18 | 36 | 54 | 72 | 90 | 108 | 126 | 144 | 162 | 180 |

pages

Ratios and Proportions

Rate

How many pickles would Justin have eaten in 10 minutes ?

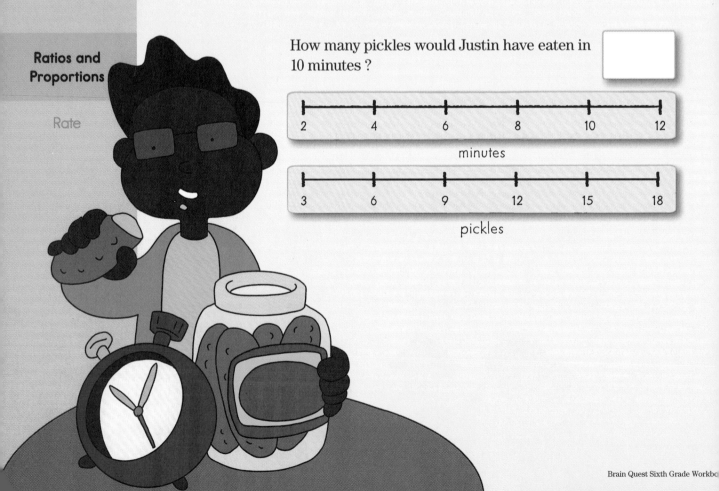

| 2 | 4 | 6 | 8 | 10 | 12 |

minutes

| 3 | 6 | 9 | 12 | 15 | 18 |

pickles

What's the Point?

Find the coordinates of each point.

1

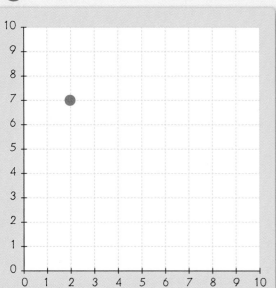

$x =$ _____ $y =$ _____

2

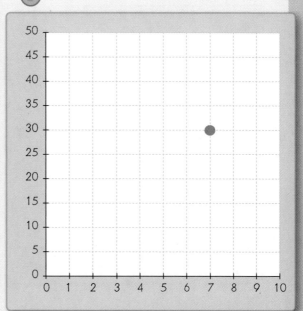

$x =$ _____ $y =$ _____

3

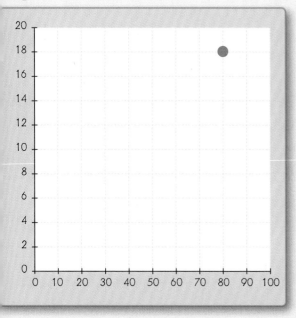

$x =$ _____ $y =$ _____

4

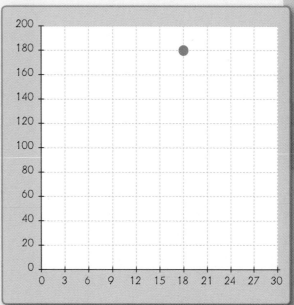

$x =$ _____ $y =$ _____

Ratios and Proportions

Graphing

Brain Box

The **x-axis** is the horizontal line. The numbers get larger as they move away from zero from left to right.

The **y-axis** is the vertical line. The numbers get larger as they move away from zero from bottom to top.

Plot the Point

Write the coordinates of each plotted point as (x,y).

1

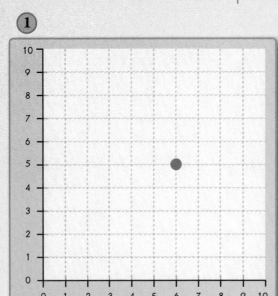

_____

2

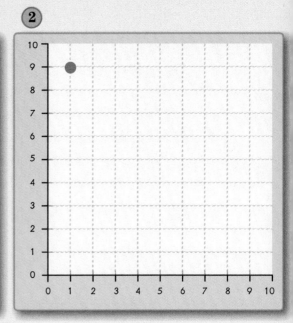

_____

Ratios and Proportions

Graphing

3

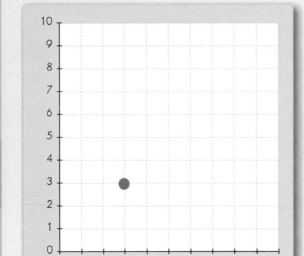

_____

4

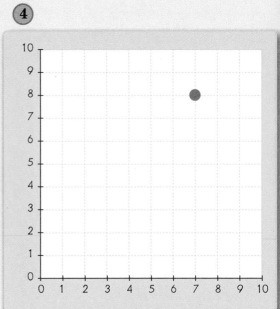

_____

①

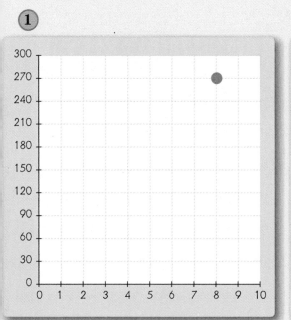

_____

②

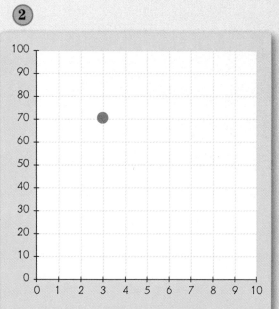

_____

③

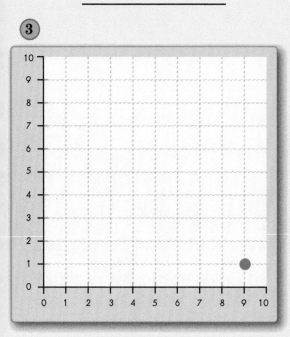

_____

④

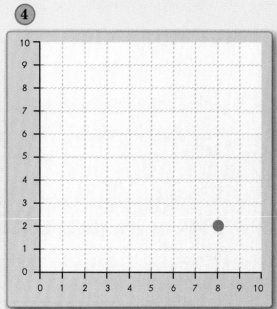

_____

Ratios and Proportions

Graphing

Manipulating Measurements

Write the answer that expresses the relationship between each set of measurements.

There are 100 centimeters in a meter.
What fraction of a meter is a centimeter?

There are 16 ounces in a pound.
What fraction of a pound is an ounce?

There are 3 teaspoons in a tablespoon.
What fraction of a tablespoon is a teaspoon?

There are 4 quarts in a gallon.
What fraction of a gallon is 2 quarts?

There are 12 inches in a foot and 3 feet in a yard.
How many inches are there in a yard?

Taking the Measure

Answer the questions.

Joe needs to add $\frac{1}{2}$ cup of water to his cake mix, but all he has to measure with is a teaspoon. There are 48 teaspoons in a cup. How many teaspoons of water does Joe need to add to his mix?

Andrea wants to mark off a quarter-mile course for a race, but all she has is a yardstick. There are 1,760 yards in a mile. How many yards does Andrea need to measure for her race course?

Allie has been saving quarters for a year. Now she wants to buy her mom a present that costs $50.75 including tax. How many quarters does Allie need to bring?

Ben is picking cherries to make jam. Each cherry weighs about $\frac{1}{2}$ ounce. There are 16 ounces in a pound. He needs 3 pounds of cherries. About how many cherries does he need to pick?

Ratios and Proportions

Conversions

Brain Box

Often, we can measure an amount in several different units.

For example, we can talk about time in terms of seconds, minutes, hours, days, years, and even centuries.

When we change the unit we use to measure something—from minutes to hours, for instance—that's called **conversion**.

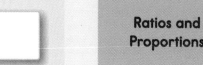

An Interesting Experiment

Scientist A is using the standard amount of food for her culture, and getting the standard rate of growth. Scientist B is performing an experiment. She uses twice as much food, and her cultures have started growing three times as fast.

Complete each table by filling in the missing numbers.

SCIENTIST A

OUNCES OF FOOD	NUMBER OF CELLS
	100
2	200
3	
4	400
	500

SCIENTIST B

OUNCES OF FOOD	NUMBER OF CELLS
2	300
	600
6	
8	1,200

Ratios and Proportions

Tables and ratios

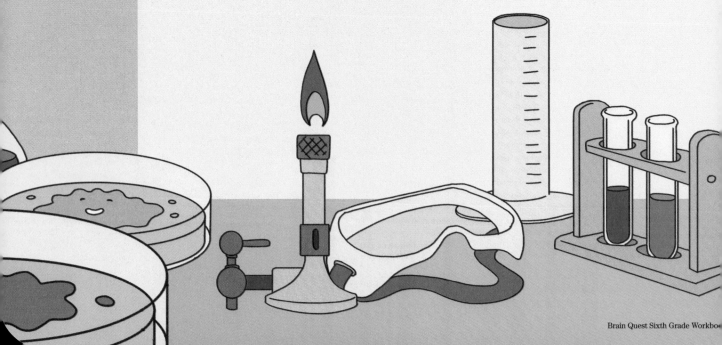

How Does It Look?

Plot the scientists' results on the graphs. Draw lines to connect the points.

SCIENTIST A

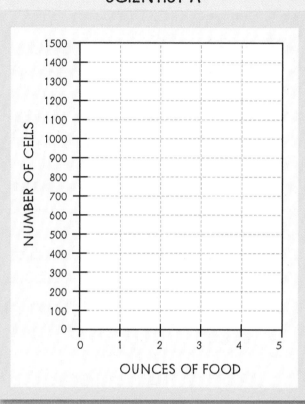

SCIENTIST B

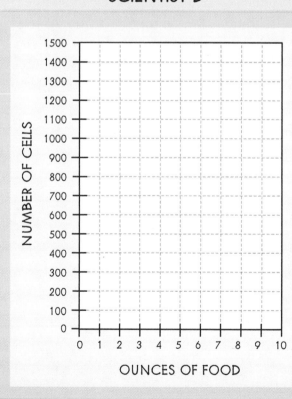

Ratios and Proportions

Graphing ratios

Quick Change

Answer the questions.

Jennifer wants to divide a gallon of milk equally among 16 students. There are 128 ounces in a gallon. How many ounces should she pour in each glass? _____

Adam spends an hour practicing the violin every day for 312 days. At the end of that time, how many 12-hour practice sessions will he have accomplished? _____

During the change drive, Oliver collected 181 pennies, 52 dimes, 28 nickels, and 13 quarters. How much money did he collect? _____

Beth has 3 yards of fabric. She wants to make scarves for 6 of her friends. There are 36 inches in a yard. How many inches of fabric can she use for each scarf? _____

Kevin likes to eat nuts and drop the shells out of the window to the roof below. He eats a lot of nuts, and the roof isn't very strong. The roof can only hold 300 pounds of weight. Each shell weighs about 1 ounce. There are 16 ounces in a pound. How many shells will it take to collapse the roof? _____

Bonus: If Kevin eats 50 nuts every day, how long will it be until the roof collapses?

_____

The
Number
System

A Piece of a Piece

Divide.

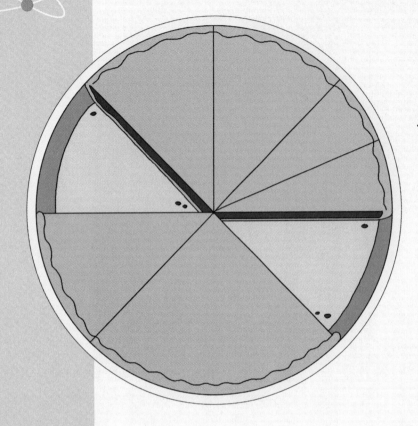

$\frac{2}{3} \div \frac{3}{4}$

$\frac{8}{10} \div \frac{1}{2}$

$\frac{4}{7} \div \frac{1}{3}$

$\frac{1}{4} \div \frac{1}{5}$

$\frac{1}{8} \div \frac{2}{5}$

Solve.

How many $\frac{1}{3}$-cup servings are in $\frac{1}{2}$ cup of whipped cream?

How much pie does each person get if 5 people share $\frac{3}{4}$ of a pie?

The Number System

Dividing fractions

Brain Box

To divide fractions, turn the second fraction upside down and multiply it by the first fraction:

$$\frac{a}{b} \div \frac{c}{d} = \frac{a}{b} \times \frac{d}{c}$$

Doing Decimals

Add.

1.25 + 2.33 =

14.7 + 21.27 =

51.23 + 189.2 =

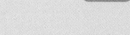

Subtract.

7.3 − 3.4 =

18.45 − 7.81 =

200.1 − 65.2 =

Multiply.

10.2 × 7.8 =

54.13 × 4.3 =

38.6 × 134.9 =

Divide.

10.25 ÷ 0.25 =

8.6 ÷ 4 =

19.5 ÷ 0.15 =

The Number System

Decimals

That's Great!

Find the **greatest common factor** of each pair of numbers.

5, 75 _____

24, 54 _____

72, 81 _____

22, 88 _____

48, 72 _____

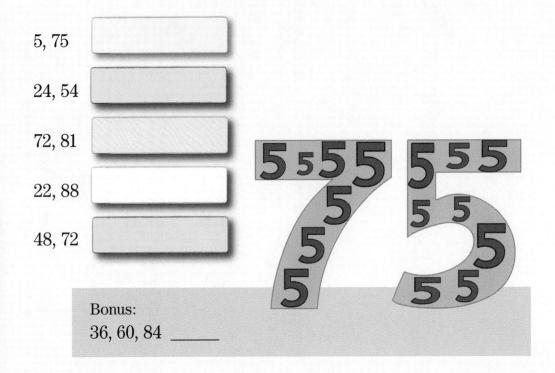

Bonus:
36, 60, 84 _____

Now that you know the greatest common factor, use the distributive property to express each pair of numbers as an equation.

For example, if the greatest common factor of 14 and 21 is 7, we can express 14 + 21 as 7(2) + 7(3) or 7(2 + 3).

5 + 75 = _____ = _____

24 − 54 = _____ = _____

72 + 81 = _____ = _____

22 + 88 = _____ = _____

48 − 72 = _____ = _____

At Least

Draw a line from each pair of numbers to their **least common multiple**.

4, 10	9
8, 6	60
7, 4	12
3, 9	20
2, 5	24
5, 12	33
6, 7	42
10, 5	28
12, 4	10
11, 3	

Bonus: Which two pairs of numbers have the same least common multiple?

_____

The Number System

Least common multiple

Brain Box

A **multiple** is a number that is the product of a given number and some other number. For instance, 4, 8, 12, and 16 are all multiples of 4. The **least common multiple** is the smallest multiple that two or more numbers have in common. For instance, 20 is the least common multiple of both 4 and 5. 20 can be divided by both 4 and 5 with no remainder.

Negative Capability

Mark the location of each number on the number line.

5

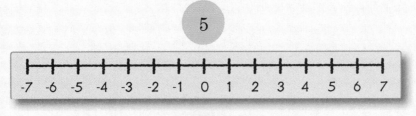

-3

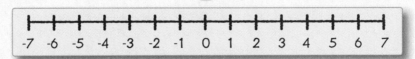

2.5

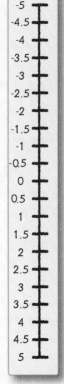

-7

O 10 100

Write the number indicated on each number line.

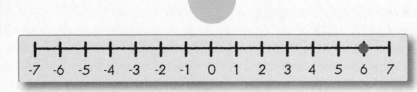

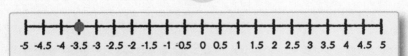

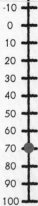

The Number System

Negative numbers

Brain Box

On a horizontal number line, positive numbers run 1, 2, 3, 4, . . . from left to right away from 0. Negative numbers run -1, -2, -3, -4, . . . from right to left away from 0.

How Coordinated Are You?

Plot the location of each point.

(3, 3)

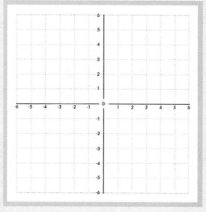

(−3, −4)

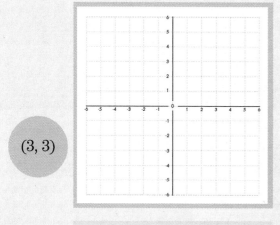

(4, −45)

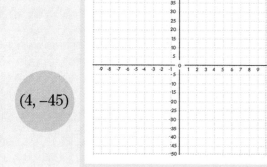

(1, −2)

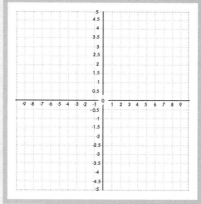

Write the coordinates of each point.

$x =$

$y =$

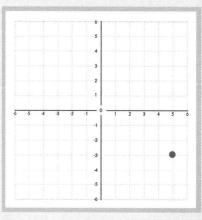

$x =$

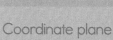

$y =$

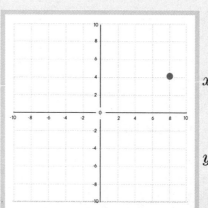

The Number System

Coordinate plane

$x =$

$y =$

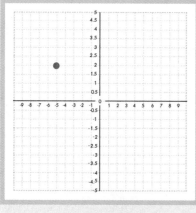

$x =$

$y =$

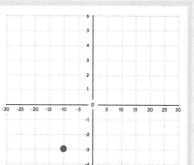

Opposites Attract

Write the opposite of each number. Then plot both numbers on the number line.

5, _____

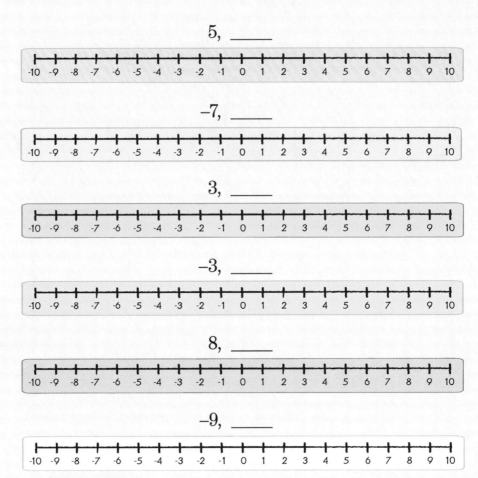

-10 -9 -8 -7 -6 -5 -4 -3 -2 -1 0 1 2 3 4 5 6 7 8 9 10

−7, _____

-10 -9 -8 -7 -6 -5 -4 -3 -2 -1 0 1 2 3 4 5 6 7 8 9 10

3, _____

-10 -9 -8 -7 -6 -5 -4 -3 -2 -1 0 1 2 3 4 5 6 7 8 9 10

−3, _____

-10 -9 -8 -7 -6 -5 -4 -3 -2 -1 0 1 2 3 4 5 6 7 8 9 10

8, _____

-10 -9 -8 -7 -6 -5 -4 -3 -2 -1 0 1 2 3 4 5 6 7 8 9 10

−9, _____

-10 -9 -8 -7 -6 -5 -4 -3 -2 -1 0 1 2 3 4 5 6 7 8 9 10

Bonus:
What is the opposite of zero? _____

The Number System

Negative numbers

Brain Box

A number's opposite is the same number with the opposite sign. It is located on the opposite side of 0 on the number line.

A Moment to Reflect

Write a check mark in the quadrant where each ordered pair would fall based on the signs.

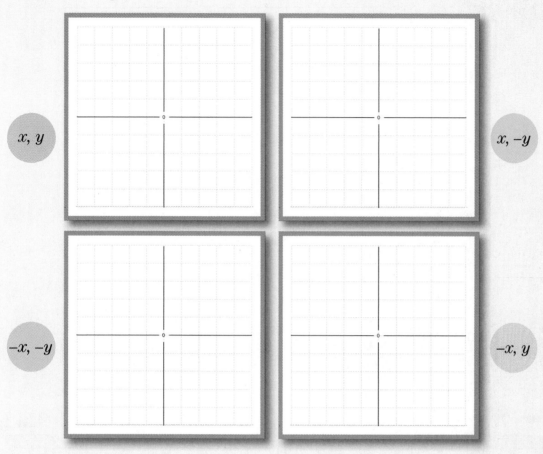

Plot each pair of mirrored ordered pairs.

The Number System

Coordinate plane

Absolutely!

Simplify.

$|7| =$ ⬜

$-|11| =$ ⬜

$|-8| =$ ⬜

$|-9 \times 2| =$ ⬜

$|5 - 2| =$ ⬜

$|4 \times 11| =$ ⬜

$|2 - 5| =$ ⬜

$-|-6| =$ ⬜

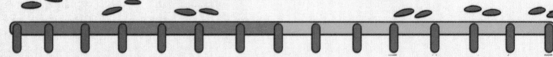

Now write each of your answers in the order they would appear on the number line.

⬜

The Number System

Absolute value

Brain Box

Absolute value is how far a number is from 0 on the number line—regardless of whether it is positive or negative. For example $|7|$ and $|-7|$ both have an absolute value of 7 because they are seven units from 0.

Get in Line

Write <, >, or = between the numbers. Then plot both numbers on the number line.

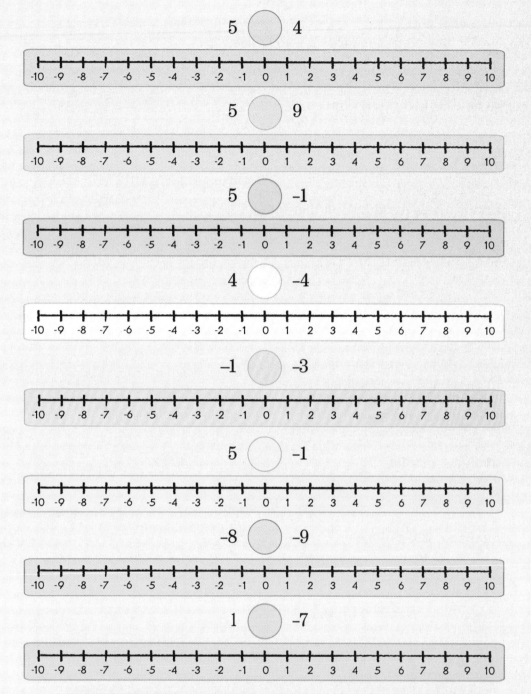

5 ◯ 4

-10 -9 -8 -7 -6 -5 -4 -3 -2 -1 0 1 2 3 4 5 6 7 8 9 10

5 ◯ 9

-10 -9 -8 -7 -6 -5 -4 -3 -2 -1 0 1 2 3 4 5 6 7 8 9 10

5 ◯ -1

-10 -9 -8 -7 -6 -5 -4 -3 -2 -1 0 1 2 3 4 5 6 7 8 9 10

4 ◯ -4

-10 -9 -8 -7 -6 -5 -4 -3 -2 -1 0 1 2 3 4 5 6 7 8 9 10

-1 ◯ -3

-10 -9 -8 -7 -6 -5 -4 -3 -2 -1 0 1 2 3 4 5 6 7 8 9 10

5 ◯ -1

-10 -9 -8 -7 -6 -5 -4 -3 -2 -1 0 1 2 3 4 5 6 7 8 9 10

-8 ◯ -9

-10 -9 -8 -7 -6 -5 -4 -3 -2 -1 0 1 2 3 4 5 6 7 8 9 10

1 ◯ -7

-10 -9 -8 -7 -6 -5 -4 -3 -2 -1 0 1 2 3 4 5 6 7 8 9 10

The Number System

Comparing numbers

Bonus: The larger number is always on which side of the smaller number? _____

Brain Box

You can think of the "greater than" or "less than" symbol as a hungry alligator. It opens its mouth wide toward whichever number is bigger.

Everything in Order

In what order do these numbers go in the following sentences? Write each sentence as a mathematical expression.

Example: 100 dollars is more than 10 dollars. $\$100 > \$10$

30 miles is less than 35 miles. _____

50 degrees Celsius is warmer than –2 degrees Celsius. _____

1 gram is heavier than 1 milligram. _____

50 cents is more than 1 cent. _____

Write a sentence that explains each mathematical expression.

12 ducklings > 2 ducklings

_____

15 mph < 70 mph

_____

1 gallon < 200 gallons

_____

The Number System

3 pizzas > 1 pizza

_____

Writing expressions

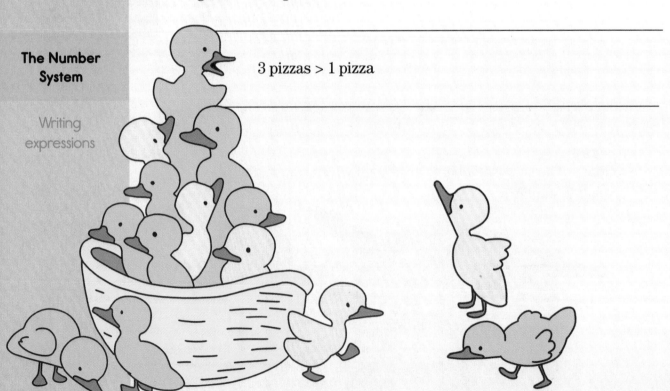

Distance from Zero

Tell how far from zero each number is on the number line.

14 [ ]   7 [ ]   −|14| [ ]

−7 [ ] |−14| [ ]

Express each question as a mathematical expression.

Joe is an hour late to class. How late is Joe to class?

_____

Kim's bank balance is ten dollars below zero. How much does Kim owe the bank?

_____

Carmen has eaten four of her sister's candy bars. How many candy bars does she need to buy to replace them?

_____

The Number System

Writing expressions

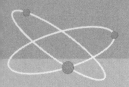

Find Your Friend

Imagine you've gone out to look for your friend—but your friend is always one step ahead of you.

Plot your location and your friend's location on each coordinate plane until you catch up!

You: at home   4, 3

Your friend: at the pool   5, 3

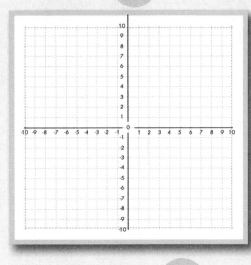

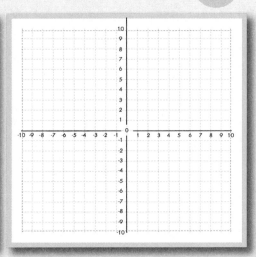

You: outside the pool   −4, 8

Your friend: at the library   −5, −4

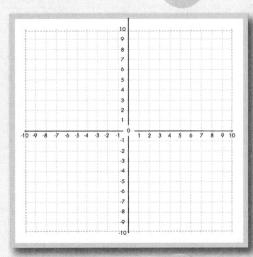

The Number System

Coordinate plane

You: near the library   −5, −2

Your friend: on the way to the park   −3, 2

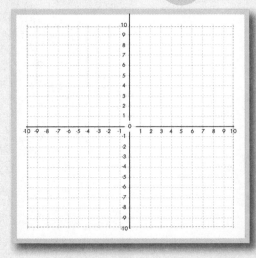

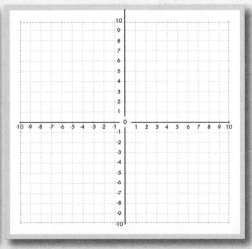

How Far Are We?

Plot each pair of points.

A

1, 1

5, 1

B

5, 1

5, –3

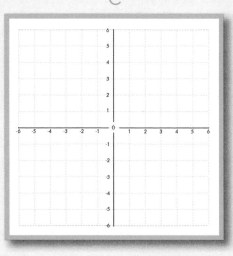

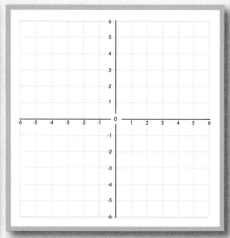

C

–5, –3

–5, 4

D

–3, 2

3, 2

Now write the number of units the two points are from one another.

A =_____   B = _____   C = _____   D = _____

The Number System

Coordinate plane

NEXT TOWN 31

Expanded Forms

Write each number in expanded form.

$2^3 =$

$4^5 =$

$10^2 =$

$5^7 =$

Write each expanded number as a single number with an exponent.

$12 \times 12 \times 12 =$

$7 \times 7 \times 7 \times 7 \times 7 =$

$125 \times 125 =$

$2 \times 2 \times 2 \times 2 \times 2 \times 2 \times 2 =$

Find the value of each number.

$10^3 =$

$100^2 =$

$2^5 =$

$4^4 =$

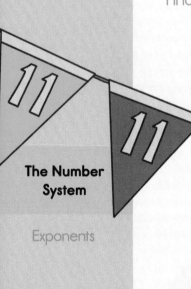

The Number System

Exponents

Brain Box

To find the value of a number with an **exponent**, multiply the number by itself as many times as the exponent shows.

Expressions and Equations

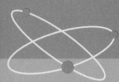

The Spice of Life

The chef is trying to clean up his kitchen, but it's a bit of a mess. Help him by writing each sentence as a mathematical expression.

The amount of spice in bottle A is greater than the amount of spice in bottle B.

If we add 1 tablespoon to the amount of spice in bottle B, it will equal the amount of spice in bottle A.

Two bottles of spice C plus one bottle of spice D equals 1 cup.

Now he's found his teaspoons and measuring cups, so he can assign values to some of his variables. Help him out by finding the value of each expression.

Brain Box

A **variable** represents a number we don't know yet. We usually write a variable as a letter. And it doesn't matter what letter we pick! We can use any one we want.

Expressions and Equations

Mathematical expressions

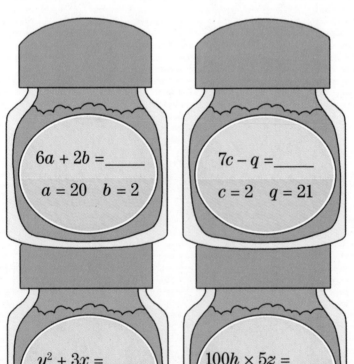

$6a + 2b = $_____
$a = 20 \quad b = 2$

$7c - q = $_____
$c = 2 \quad q = 21$

$y^2 + 3x = $_____
$y = 3 \quad x = 11$

$100h \times 5z = $_____
$h = 9 \quad z = 0$

$(4g + 5y)^2 = $_____
$g = 10 \quad y = 6$

Shorthand

Write each sentence as a mathematical expression.

Reporter's Notebook

Add 5 and a. _____

Subtract 10 from b. _____

Multiply 5 by a. _____

Divide 7 by b. _____

Add a and b. _____

Multiply a by b. _____

Add a and b, then multiply the sum by 5. _____

Add b and 5, then divide the sum by a. _____

Expressions
and Equations

Writing
expressions

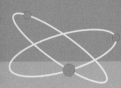

190

Vocabulary—for Math!

Answer the questions.

$$5(x + y) - 3(\tfrac{y}{x})$$

What is the sum in this expression? _____

What is the quotient? _____

How many coefficients are there? _____

What are they? _____

$$3 + ab + 5xy$$

How many terms are in this expression? _____

What are they? _____

What are the factors of $5xy$? _____

How many products are there in this expression? _____

What are they? _____

What is the coefficient of $5xy$? _____

$$3(5 + 6)$$

How many products are there in this expression? _____

How many factors are there in this expression? _____

Expressions and Equations

Math vocabulary

Brain Box

A **sum** is the result of adding two or more numbers and/or variables.

A **term** is a part of an expression set off by + or –. It can be a number, a variable, variables multiplied together, or numbers and variables multiplied together.

A **product** is the result of multiplying two or more numbers and/or variables.

A **factor** is a number that can be divided into another number with no remainder.

A **quotient** is the result of dividing two numbers and/or variables.

A **coefficient** is the number that a variable is multiplied by.

Construction Site

Answer the questions.

Each construction block is 12 inches wide, 15 inches long, and 5 inches tall. What is the surface area of each block? (Hint: Find the area of each of the block's six faces, then add them together.)

_____

What is the volume of each block?

_____

The four walls in the dining room are each 20 feet by 10 feet. The windows take up 30 square feet, and the doors take up another 50 square feet. How many square feet of wall space is there in the dining room?

_____

The closet has no windows and only three walls. All walls are the same size, so their total area equals 3(*lw*). What is the total surface area of the walls of the closet if each wall is 10 feet long and 3 feet wide?

_____

It takes 1 pail of paint to cover 300 square feet. How many pails will it take to paint the dining room and closet? (Express your answer in decimal form.)

_____

_____

The paint rollers are delivered in cubic cardboard boxes, which means their length, width, and height are all equal. What is their volume if the length of one side of a box is 10 inches?

_____

_____

_____

Expressions and Equations

Values and variables

Work It Out

Use the values of the variables to simplify each expression. If the simplified form is not a whole number, express it as a decimal.

$a = 3$	$b = 4$	$c = \dfrac{1}{2}$	$d = 100$

$\dfrac{ab}{d} = \dfrac{74}{100}$

solution:

$104 - 3\frac{1}{2} = 101\frac{1}{2}$

$(d + b) - ac$

solution: $101\frac{1}{2}$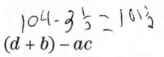

$\begin{array}{r} 3 \\ 96 \\ \times \; 5 \\ \hline 480 \end{array}$ 5×96

$5(d - b)$

solution: 480

c^a

solution:

---

b^2

solution: 8

$7bc - (a + b)$

$14 - 7 = 7$

solution: 7

$\dfrac{(a - c)}{b}$

solution:

$\dfrac{db}{c^b}$

solution:

Find the Equal

Circle the pairs in which the equal expressions are equivalent.

ab and $a + b$

a^3 and $3a$

$b(a + c)$ and $ab + bc$

$\dfrac{5 - y}{5}$ and $\dfrac{1 - y}{5}$

$b + b + b + a$ and $b^3 + a$

$3(b + b + b + a)$ and $9b + 3a$

$5ab - 2ab$ and $3ab$

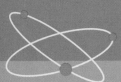

Spare Ribs

This family loves ribs. Their dad also loves keeping notes, but his notes aren't very good.

Construct a table that shows how many ribs, how much cole slaw, and how much iced tea the family consumed in each month of the year based on these jumbled jottings.

Iced Tea
  March: 7 gal.
  April: 7 gal.
  May: 8 gal.

Iced Tea, January: 2
Ribs, January: 204
Jan. Cole Slaw: 10 lbs.
Ribs, June: 440
Ribs, July: 518
Ribs, Aug: 650
Ribs, Sept: 395
Ribs, Oct: 401
Ribs, Nov: 451

December
  Ribs: 793
  Iced Tea: 13 gal.
  Cole Slaw: 3 lbs.

February
  Ribs: 267
  Cole Slaw: 9 lbs.
  Iced Tea: 3 gal.

March
  Ribs: 325
  Cole Slaw: 8 lbs.

April
  Ribs: 375
  Cole Slaw: 7 lbs.

May
  Ribs: 408
  Cole Slaw: 5 lbs.

June Cole Slaw: 5 lbs.
July Cole Slaw: 4.5 lbs.
Aug. Cole Slaw: 4 lbs.
Sept. Cole Slaw: 6 lbs.
Oct. Cole Slaw: 6 lbs.
Nov. Cole Slaw: 5 lbs.

Month	Ribs	Cole Slaw	Iced Tea

Iced Tea

June : 10 gal.
July : 10 gal.
Aug : 11 gal.
Sept : 9 gal.
Oct : 9 gal.
Nov : 8 gal.

Expressions and Equations

Creating tables

Reading the Signs

Use the table you constructed on the previous page to answer the questions.

In what month did the family consume the most ribs?

_____

In what month did the family drink the most iced tea?

_____

In what month did the family eat the most cole slaw?

_____

In what month did the family eat the fewest ribs?

_____

When the family ate more cole slaw, did they eat more or fewer ribs?

_____

When the family ate more ribs, did they drink more or less iced tea?

_____

**Expressions
and Equations**

Reading tables

Keep It Equal

A mathematical operation has been performed on one side of the equal sign in each equation. Determine what the operation was, then perform it on the other side of the equal sign to keep everything equal.

Original Equation

Equivalent Equation

$x + y = 2x$

$5x + 5y =$ ____

$a - b = bc$

$8(a - b) =$ ____

$xy = ab$

$xy + 2 =$ ____

$5(x - y)^3 = xy + 5$

$5(x - y)^3 - 3 =$ ____

Expressions and Equations

Properties of equality

Brain Box

No matter what mathematical operation we perform, as long as we do it on both sides of the equal sign, the equation remains true.

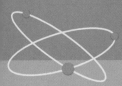

Brain Box

The **distributive property** says that when we multiply an expression inside parentheses by a given number, it's the same as individually multiplying each term of the expression by that number. For example, a(b+c) =

a x b + a x c
or a(b+c) =
ab + ac

Expressions and Equations

Distributive property

Distribution Operation

Solve or simplify the problems. Use the distributive property when necessary.

$5(1 + 2) =$

$7(14 + 25)$

$11(x + 10) =$

$y + y + y + x + x + 3 =$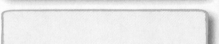

$8(3x + 4y) =$

$x(5 + 6) =$

$x(x + y) =$

$4x(10 + x + y) =$

$9(7x + y + y + 5 + z^3 + y) =$

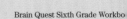

Equal Amounts

Substitute the values of the variables in each equation.
Then circle the ones that are true (both sides of the equal sign are
in fact equal).

$$a = 1 \qquad b = 5 \qquad c = 7$$

$ab = c$

$2a + b = c$

$4b = 3 - c - 1$

$a^2 = 2a$

$10b = 100a$

$\dfrac{b}{a} = c - 2a$

$a(b + c) = b + c$

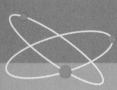
Various Variables

Read these descriptions of real-life situations. Then determine whether the solution to the problem would be a single value or a set of values.

Vince's older sister bought 48 hot dogs and buns for his birthday. He doesn't care how many kids come to his party, as long as each of them get a hot dog. How many kids can come to his party?

_____

Davesh wants to make a stained-glass window for his mom's room as a present. So he has to measure the original window carefully. If the stained glass he makes is too big, it won't fit. And if it's too small, it won't work as a window. How much glass does Davesh need?

_____

Ava's mom is making costumes for the school play. She needs to make 3 blue capes, and she has 7 yards of fabric. Each cape requires at least a yard of fabric. But she could also use more fabric in each cape to make them more spectacular. If all three capes must be the same size, how much fabric can she use per cape?

_____

Alvin broke his shoelace. He needs to replace it with one that's exactly the same length. How long should his new shoelace be?

_____

_____

Brain Box

Some variables stand for just one number; if we substitute anything else into the equation, it will no longer be true.

But sometimes several different numbers can be used in the equation, and it will still be true. When that occurs, we call that group of numbers a **solution set**.

Charitable Solutions

Write each problem as an equation using the variables x, y, and z.
Then substitute the variables with the given values and solve the equation.

Tom brought 7 coats to the shelter, and Marisol brought twice
as many as that. How many coats did they bring in all? If the
number of coats is your variable, write and solve the equation.

Equation: _____

Substitution: _____

Solution: _____

Lee serves 2 cups of hot soup every minute. If he works for
30 minutes, how many cups of soup will he have passed out?

Equation: _____

Substitution: _____

Solution: _____

Shawna's student read 15 pages during their tutoring session,
and Brandon's student read 3 more than that. How many pages
did they read in all?

Equation: _____

Substitution: _____

Solution: _____

The health clinic never closes. Fifty-five people come to the clinic
every day. How many people come to the clinic in a single week?

Equation: _____

Substitution: _____

Solution: _____

Brain Box

When we
make a
substitution,
we replace a
variable with
a number we
know.
Then we can
solve the
problem!

**Expressions
and Equations**

Word problems

It Depends

Write each sentence as an equation.

Shaunte makes sure to run twice as fast as her little sister Cherise.

_____

No matter how many push-ups Tim does, Jasper always says he's done one more.

_____

It takes the team bus an hour to travel 60 miles.

_____

Each player drinks three glasses of water every hour they practice.

_____

Talking Tables

Use the information on the previous page to complete each table.

Shaunte	Cherise
	1 mph
4 mph	
6 mph	
	4 mph

Tim	Jasper
1 push-up	2 push-ups
	6 push-ups
	8 push-ups
10 push-ups	

Hours	Miles
	60
2	120
3	
	300

Hours	Glasses of Water/Player
1	
2	
4	

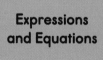

Expressions and Equations

Dependent variables

Dependable Trends

Use the tables on the previous page to complete each graph. Draw a line to connect each point.

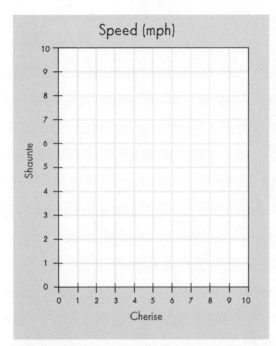

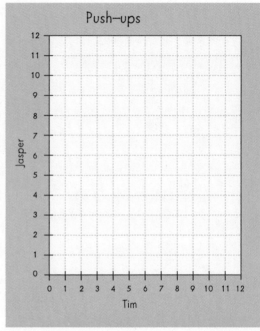

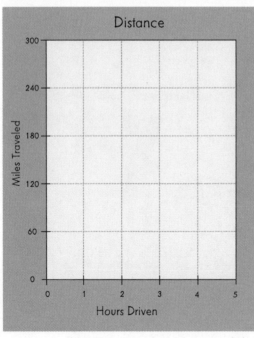

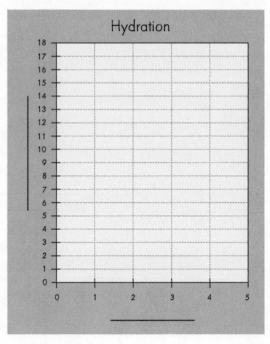

Bonus: What should the x- and y-axes on the Hydration graph be labeled?

x-axis: _____

y-axis: _____

Geometry

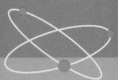

The Volume of Volumes

Find the area of each front cover and the volume of each book.

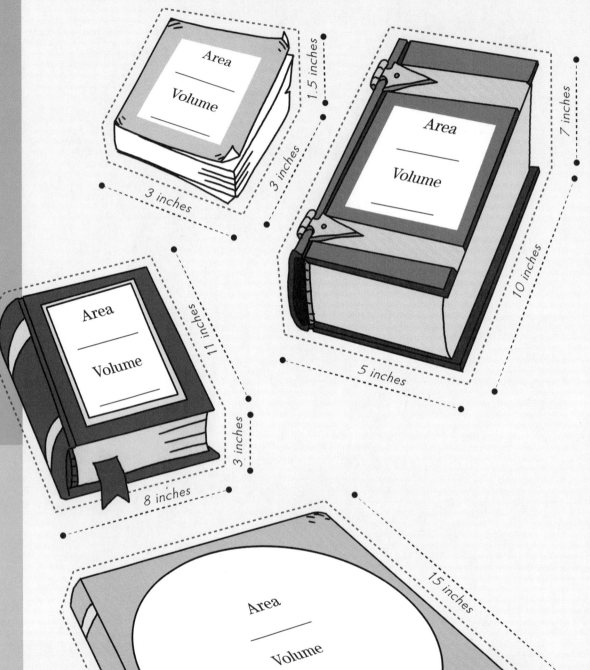

Area
___
Volume

1.5 inches

3 inches

3 inches

Area
___
Volume
___

7 inches

10 inches

5 inches

Area
___
Volume

11 inches

3 inches

8 inches

Area
___
Volume
___

15 inches

1 inch

10 inches

Brain Box

The **area** of a rectangle is A = length × width.

The **volume** of a rectangular solid is V = length × width × height.

Geometry

Area and volume

The Right Area

Find the area, surface area, or volume of each shape.

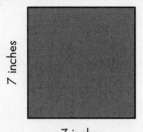

7 inches

7 inches

area _____

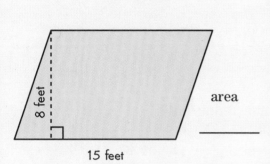

8 feet

15 feet

area _____

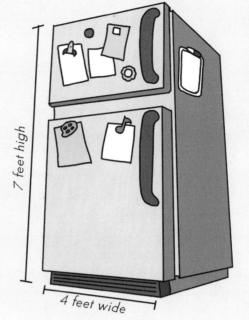

7 feet high

4 feet wide

area _____

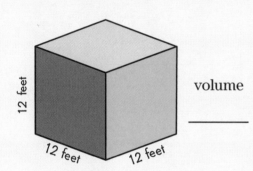

12 feet

12 feet   12 feet

volume _____

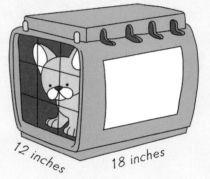

18 inches

12 inches   18 inches

volume _____

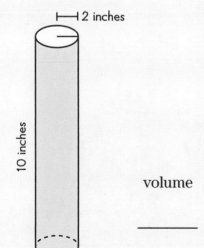

2 inches

10 inches

volume _____

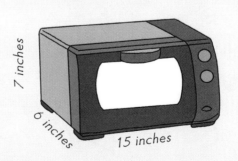

7 inches

6 inches   15 inches

volume _____

Brain Box

The volume of a cylinder is $V = \pi r^2 h$.

Don't forget $\pi \approx 3.14$.

Geometry

Area and volume

Bonus: Express the volume of the toaster oven in cubic feet instead of cubic inches. _____

A Problem of Volume

Solve.

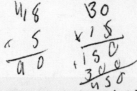

$C6$

Mrs. Cervantes wants to paint her windmill. It has 6 sides, each of which is 3.5 feet wide by 11 feet tall. How many square feet does she need to paint?

$2265.05f$

Raj's little brother just got a new toy box. It is 3 feet wide, 5 feet deep, and 6 feet long. How many cubic feet of storage space does it have?

$90 ft^3$

Jesse needs a new rug. The space on her floor is 7 feet long by 6 feet wide. She found a rug she loves that is 55 square feet. Will it fit on her floor?

No

Angie wants to fill the kiddie pool with table tennis balls. The kiddie pool is 3 feet deep, 10 feet wide, and 15 feet long. How many cubic feet of table-tennis-ball space does she have?

$450 ft^3$

Bonus: Each table tennis ball takes up 2 cubic inches of space. How many table tennis balls does she need? ___225___

225

Geometry

Area and volume

Triangles and Rectangles

For each **right triangle**, draw two lines to create another right triangle, and show how every triangle is really half of a square or rectangle. Then find the area of the original triangle. If the area is not a whole number, express it as a decimal.

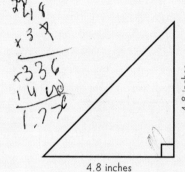

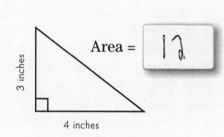

Area = 25 sq. in.

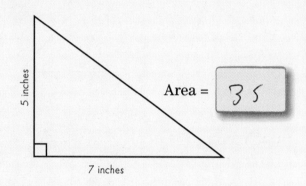

Area = 17.6

Area = 12

Area = 35

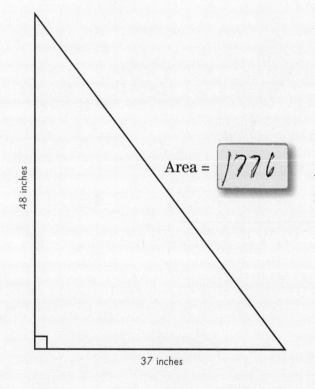

Area = 1776

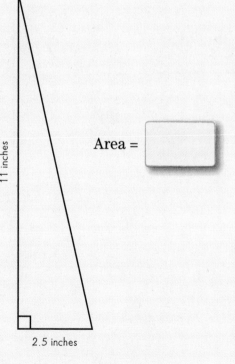

Area =

Area = 8

Brain Box

The area of a right triangle equals half the product of the lengths of its legs, or

$$A = \frac{ab}{2}$$

That's because the area of a right triangle is always half the area of a square or rectangle.

Geometry

Area of triangles

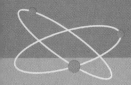

Two Triangles

Draw three lines in each triangle to create right triangles.

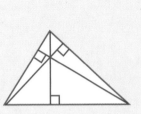

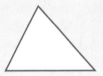

Find the area of each of these triangles. If the area is not a whole number, express it as a decimal.

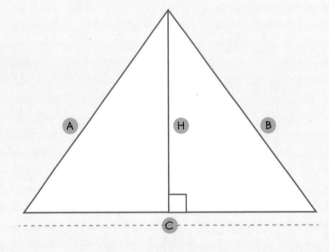

A = 5

B = 5

C = 6

H = 4

Area

_____

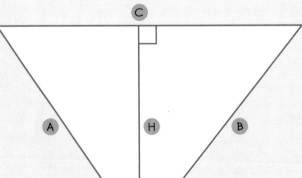

A = 17

B = 17

C = 16

H = 15

Area

_____

Sizing Up Shapes

Match each quadrilateral with the group of rectangles, squares, or right triangles that can form it.

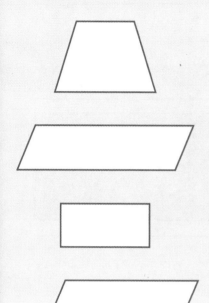

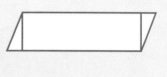

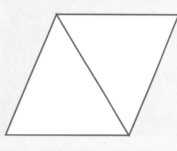

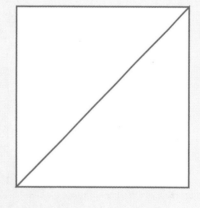

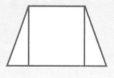

Geometry

Area of
quadrilaterals

Lawn Logic

Find the area of each irregularly shaped lawn.

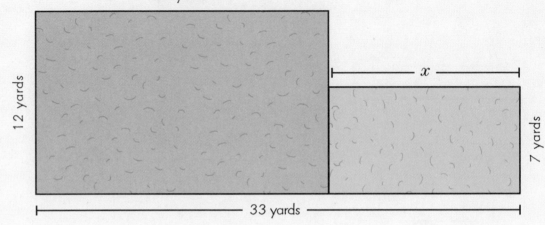

Area = _____ x = _____

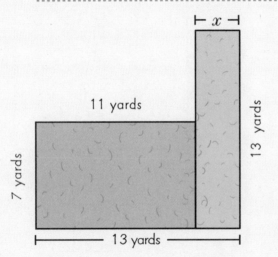

Area = _____ x = _____

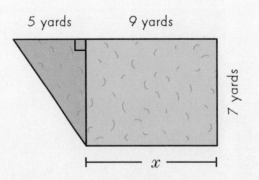

Area = _____ x = _____

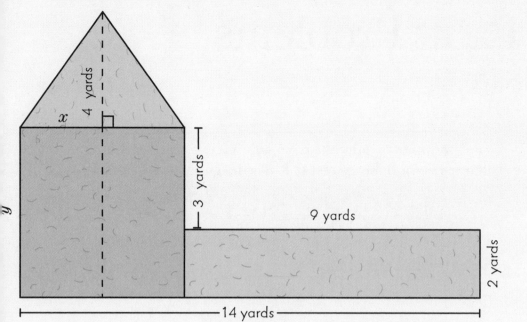

Area = _____   y = _____   x = _____

. . . .

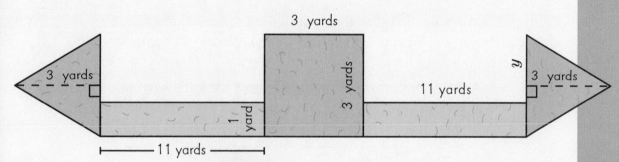

Area = _____   y = _____

. . . .

Geometry

Area

Paint Problems

Solve.

Jeanette wants to paint the triangular peak of her house a different color than the rest of it. The height of the peak is 17 feet, and the width of her whole house is 22 feet.

What calculations will Jeanette need to do to find the area of each shape?

_____

How big is the area she wants to paint?

_____

Juan wants to paint the floor of his basement. The main room is 24 feet by 15 feet, but there is also a storage room that is 3 feet by 6 feet.

What shapes does Juan want to paint?

_____

What calculations will Juan need to do to find the area of each shape?

_____

How big is the area he wants to paint?

_____

Brain Box

How do we find the area of a triangle that is not a right triangle? That formula is also simple: $A = \frac{1}{2} \times base \times height$.

Geometry

Area

Marlon wants to paint the side of a playhouse with a window in it. The side of the playhouse is 6 feet by 8 feet, and the window is 3 feet high by 1.5 feet wide.

What shapes are involved in Marlon's calculations?

_____

What calculations will Marlon need to do in order to find the area of the space he wants to paint?

_____

What is the area of the space that Marlon wants to paint?

_____

Amal is painting the main street of a model town. The street is 24 inches long by 1.5 inches wide, until it turns at an angle. The angle forms a triangle with one side of 2 inches and two sides of 1.5 inches that form a right angle. Then the street, still 1.5 inches wide, continues on for another 11 inches.

What shapes does Amal want to paint?

_____

What calculations will Amal need to do to find the area of each shape?

_____

How big is the area Amal wants to paint?

_____

Geometry

Area

Building Blocks

Draw any lines necessary to divide each shape into squares, rectangles, or triangles whose areas you can calculate. Then calculate.

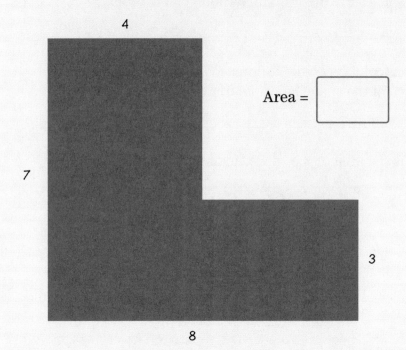

4

7

3

8

Area =

8

Area =

5

2   2

3

5

7   1

Area =

2

5

2

20

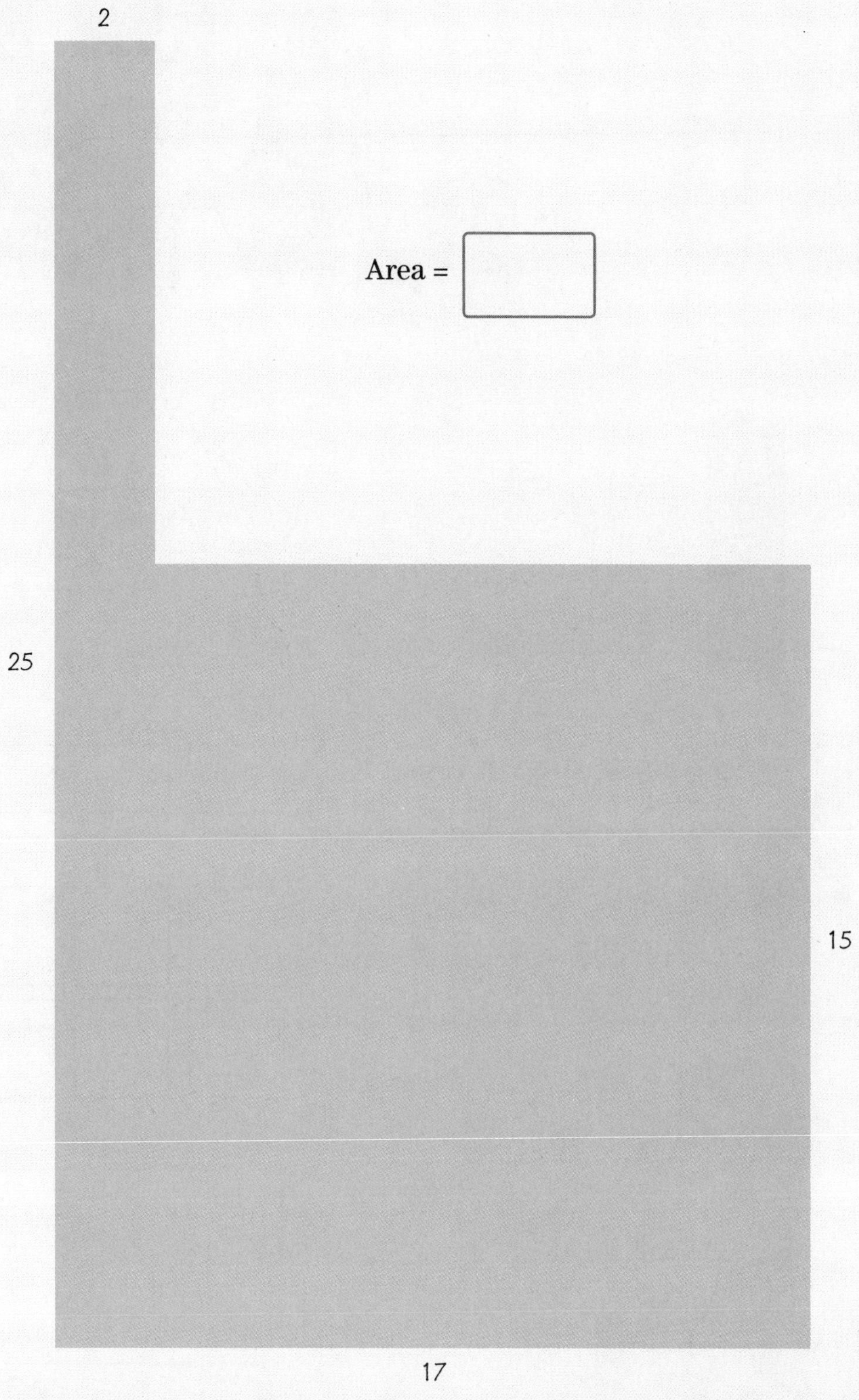

2

Area =

25

15

17

7

Area =

3

12

Area

On the Surface

Match each three-dimensional shape with the flat shapes that would be required to cover its entire exterior.

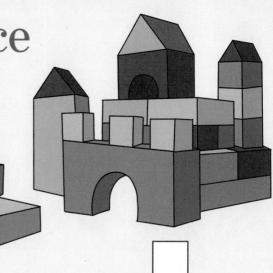

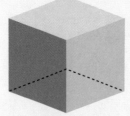

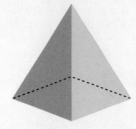

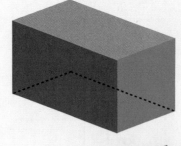

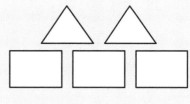

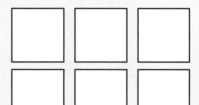

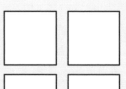

Geometry

Pack It Up!

Answer the questions.

> Philip is packing up books. Each book is 11 inches long, 8 inches wide, and 2 inches thick. His boxes are 16 inches wide, 22 inches long, and 16 inches deep.

How many books can he fit and lay flat in a single layer in a box?

_____

How many layers of books can Philip fit in a box? _____

How many books can Philip fit in one box? _____

Philip has 78 books and 2 boxes. Does he have enough boxes
for all of his books? If not, how many books will be left over? _____

What is the volume of one of Philip's books? _____

Find the volume of the books that will fit in one of Philip's boxes by
multiplying the volume of one book by the total number of books that
will fit in a box. _____

Find the volume of one of Philip's boxes. _____

How does the volume of the box compare to the total volume of the
books inside it? _____

Geometry

Volume

Candy Bar Catastrophe

Someone forgot to close the back of a truck filled with candy bars.
Answer the questions to help make sure everything gets back on the truck.

The surface area of the top of each candy bar is 17.5 square inches, and each candy bar is 0.5 inch thick. What is the volume of each candy bar?

Based on the surface area of the top, if each candy bar is 7 inches long, how wide is it?

A box of candy bars is 10 inches wide. How many candy bars can fit vertically (standing upright) in a single row along those 10 inches?

A box of candy bars is 21 inches long. How many candy bars can fit in it lengthwise (lying flat) along those 21 inches?

How many candy bars fit in a single layer (lying flat) in a box?

A box can hold 19 layers of candy bars (lying flat) with no extra room. How many inches tall is the box?

Calculate the volume of a box of candy bars in cubic inches.

The candy boxes are shipped in large cartons. Each carton is 3 feet long, 3 feet deep, and 2.5 feet tall. They can be stacked 9 boxes high inside each candy company truck with no room left over. How tall are the trucks?

The candy company trucks are 36 feet long. How many boxes does it take to form a single line of boxes along one 36-foot side?

When a trucker opens the back of a truck filled with candy bars, he sees a wall 9 cartons high and 6 cartons wide with no room left over. How wide is the back of a candy company truck?

What is the total volume of a candy company truck?

How many cartons can a candy company truck hold?

If each carton holds 18 boxes of candy bars, and each box holds 76 candy bars, how many candy bars are on each truck?

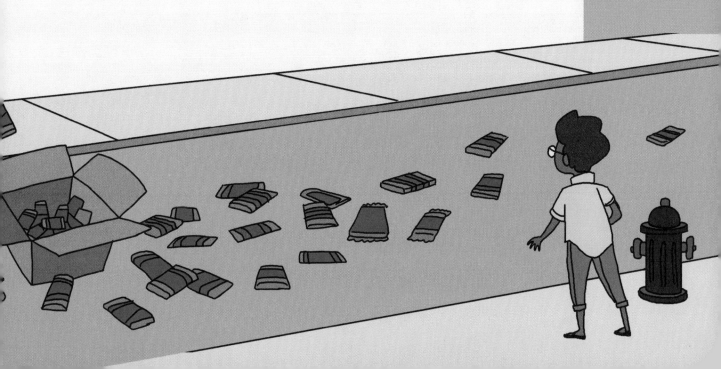

Numbers and Nets

Match each word problem with the appropriate diagram on the next page.

Gabriel bought his dad a poster that came in a triangular box. Instead of six sides, the box only has five, so that the two ends each form the shape of a triangle. What is the surface area of the box?

_____

Jordan is flattening out book boxes with rectangular sides. How much surface area will a box take up once it is flattened?

_____

Anh is building a scale model of the pyramids out of cardboard. How much cardboard will she need to complete it?

_____

Rick is building a cubic footstool that folds together from plastic sides. What is the surface area of the completed cube?

_____

Jason wants to change the color of his triangular prism by covering the sides with colored paper. How much colored paper does he need to cover the whole thing?

_____

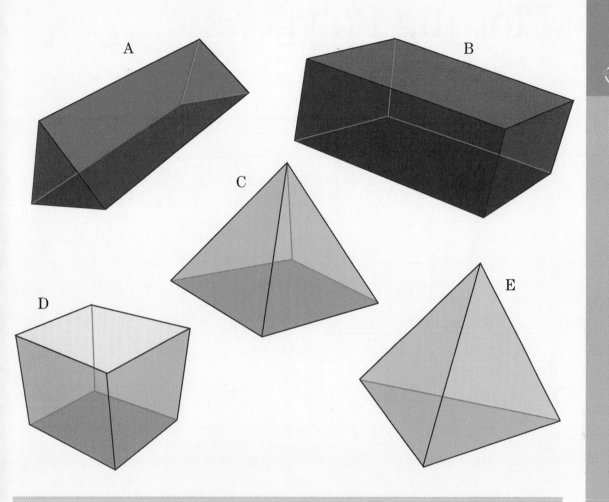

A

B

C

D

E

Bonus: Which word problem could go with more than one of the diagrams?

_____

Geometry

Surface area

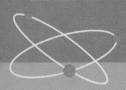

Plotting Polygons

Plot each set of points. Then identify the kind of polygon that would result if you connected the points.

1.

A	B	C
(3, –3)	(–3, –3)	(–3, 3)

shape: _____

2.

A	B	C
(1, 1)	(–3, –3)	(4, –3)

shape: _____

3.

A	B	C	D
(1, 2)	(2, 5)	(6, 2)	(5, 5)

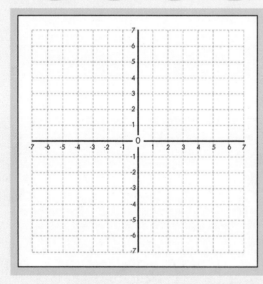

shape: _____

4.

A	B	C	D
(3, 2)	(–4, 2)	(1, –2)	(–6, –2)

shape: _____

Brain Box

When we see an "ordered pair" of numbers, what order are they in?

The first number always refers to a point on the *x*-axis, and the second number always refers to a point on the *y*-axis.

Geometry

Coordinate plane

Statistics and Probability

Is That Statistical?

Circle the statistical question(s) in each pair.

Hint: Both questions may be statistical, or neither may be!

A. How many pairs of shoes does Josh own?

B. How many pairs of shoes does each person in Josh's class own?

A. How many kids are there in each school in the district?

B. How many kids are there in Ms. Chang's class?

A. How many plants did Ginger plant in her garden?

B. How many cups of lemonade did Ginger sell at the book fair?

A. How many glasses of milk did each student drink before school?

B. How many glasses of milk did Marcus drink before school?

A. How many students ride each school bus?

B. How many students attend each lunch period?

Brain Box

A **statistical question** doesn't just have one answer.

Instead, it has many answers. Or it takes many questions to find one answer.

It Varies

Make a plan for data collection by answering the following questions.

How many people on the block have dogs?

Who would you need to ask in order to answer this question? _____

How many answers would you get? _____

Is this a statistical question? _____

How many dogs does Mrs. Singh have?

Whom would you need to ask in order to answer this question? _____

How many answers would you get? _____

Is this a statistical question? _____

Do people on the block have more black dogs or more brown dogs?

Whom would you need to ask in order to answer this question? _____

How many answers would you get? _____

Is this a statistical question? _____

Brain Box

In statistics, **variability** means how spread out the data is. A statistical question generates more than one answer.

Statistics and Probability

Variability

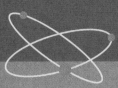

Ice Cream Statistics

Use each data set to answer the questions.

Favorite Flavor	Votes
Chocolate	21
Strawberry	7
Vanilla	3
Rocky Road	15

What is the flavor with the greatest number of votes? _____

What is the flavor with the least number of votes? _____

What is the difference between the greatest and the least number of votes?

_____

What is the number that is exactly halfway between the greatest number and the least number of votes? _____

Which flavor has the number of votes closest to that number?

_____

Statistics and Probability

Distribution

Days of the Week	Number of Customers
Monday	50
Tuesday	53
Wednesday	51
Thursday	55
Friday	75
Saturday	101
Sunday	85

What was the busiest day of the week? _____

What was the slowest day of the week? _____

What were the three slowest days of the week? _____

What were the three busiest days of the week? _____

What day has a number of customers that is closest to the number exactly halfway between the number of customers on the busiest day of the week and the number on the slowest day?

_____

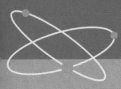

Drawing Data

Use the graphs to answer the questions.

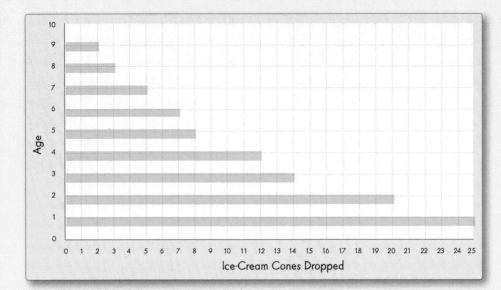

What are the middle two numbers of ice-cream cones in this data set? _____

What is the spread between the greatest number of cones dropped and the least? _____

What is the spread between the lowest age and the highest? _____

What is the shape of this data? _____

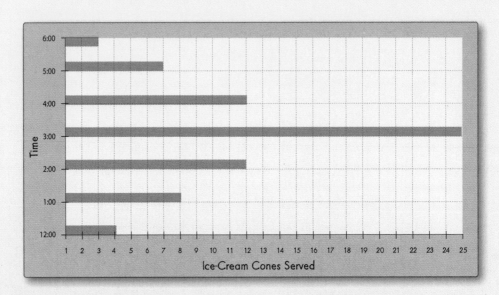

What is the middle time of day in this data set? _____

What is the greatest number of cones? _____

When does the greatest number of cones fall in this data set? _____

What is the spread between the greatest and the least number in this data set? _____

What is the shape of this data? _____

Brain Box

Often, the easiest way to see distribution is on a graph.

The center of a data set on a graph is its **midpoint**.

The **spread** of data is the range from its highest to its lowest points.

The **shape** of the data describes the way it looks when graphed.

Statistics and Probability

Graphing distribution

Dot Plots

Create a dot plot to show each data set.

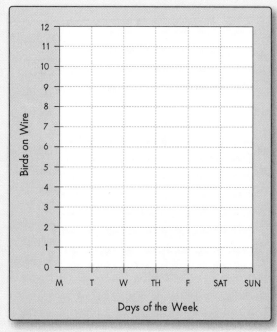

Day:	Birds on Wire
Monday:	7
Tuesday:	6
Wednesday:	8
Thursday:	11
Friday:	10
Saturday:	11
Sunday:	12

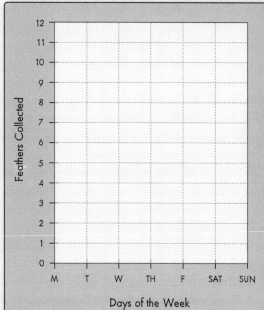

Day:	Feathers Collected
Monday:	2
Tuesday:	1
Wednesday:	5
Thursday:	3
Friday:	7
Saturday:	1
Sunday:	10

Brain Box

A **dot plot** shows information by displaying a dot for each point of data.

Statistics and Probability

Displaying data

Measurement Matters

Read the story. Then answer the questions.

Brain Box

The way data is collected, the way it's measured, and even how much data is collected all affect what we can learn from it. These circumstances form the **context**.

Dana and David are collecting data about people's favorite colors by asking strangers downtown. They got answers from 10 women, all wearing red scarves, who were having some kind of meeting at a local coffee shop. There were 6 other people in the coffee shop, but none of them would give an answer. They got answers from the 2 men working at the copy shop next door. Then they stood on the street and got answers from another 10 people. They actually stopped 20 people, but only 10 gave them answers. And while they were talking with those people, another 12 people walked by. These are their results:

Red:	11
Blue:	4
Green:	2
Yellow:	5

Statistics and Probability

Data context

How many answers did they get?

_____

How many people did they interact with?

_____

How many more people did they talk with than answered them?

_____

How many total people did they encounter, including the ones who walked by as they were interviewing other people?

_____

Divide the number of people who they got answers from by the total number of people they encountered. That gives you the percentage of people who they got answers from.

_____

Measurement Matters

Read the data on page 232. Then answer the questions.

What color is the most popular, according to their data?

_____

Are there any hints in the story that suggest that any of the people they asked might have unusual opinions about colors?

_____

What percentage of the people who answered liked the color red best?

_____

Of the people from whom they don't have answers, 18 people liked blue best, 4 people liked green best, and 6 people liked yellow best. Revise the results to include those answers:

_____

Red: [   ]

Blue: [   ]

Green: [   ]

Yellow: [   ]

Blue originally seemed a little less popular than red.

According to the new results, how many times more popular is blue than red?

_____

How to Ask

Demetrius is designing a survey to find out how much time his classmates spend doing homework. Answer the questions to help him weigh the various options for collecting data.

Ask Students

What are two advantages of asking students directly?

_____

What are two reasons that students might not give accurate data?

_____

Ask the Teacher

What are two advantages of asking the teacher?

_____

What are two reasons that the teacher might not give accurate data?

_____

Ask the Family

What are two advantages of asking a student's family?

_____

_____

What are two disadvantages of asking a student's family?

_____

Measure It

What are two advantages of taking actual measurements?

_____

What are two disadvantages of taking actual measurements?

_____

If you had to design a survey to see how much time your classmates spend doing homework, what option or options would you use? Why?

_____

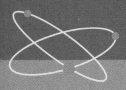

Using Units

Molly has been collecting data on how much water her cat drinks every day. She recorded her findings using three kinds of measurements. Create a bar graph from each set of measurements.

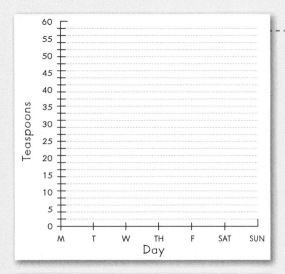

Monday :   36 teaspoons

Tuesday :   24 teaspoons

Wednesday :   60 teaspoons

Thursday :   48 teaspoons

Friday :   36 teaspoons

Saturday :   48 teaspoons

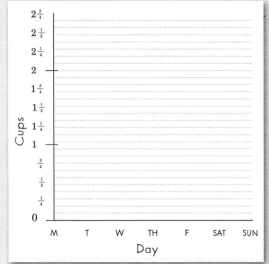

Monday: $\frac{3}{4}$ cup

Tuesday: $\frac{1}{2}$ cup

Wednesday: $1\frac{1}{4}$ cups

Thursday: 1 cup

Friday: $\frac{3}{4}$ cup

Saturday: 1 cup

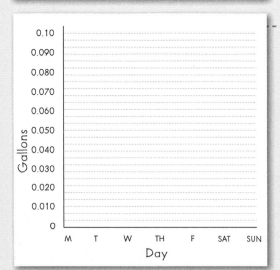

Monday: 0.047 gallons

Tuesday: 0.031 gallons

Wednesday: 0.078 gallons

Thursday: 0.062 gallons

Friday: 0.047 gallons

Saturday: 0.062 gallons

Brain Box

The units of measurement we choose to use when we collect data can affect what we're able to learn from the data.

Statistics and Probability

Mean

Bonus: What units of measurement would you choose to use for this experiment? Why?

_____

What's That Mean?

Find the mean of each group of numbers.

1; 2; 3; 4; 5; 6; 7 _____

14; 14; 15; 16; 17; 17; 17; 18 _____

204; 228; 203; 350; 400 _____

5; 897; 1; 2; 4 _____

23; 151; 239; 367; 455; 531; 688; 720; 801; 950; 1,081 _____

Answer the questions.

Kwame did 10 math problems on Monday, 26 on Tuesday, 30 on Wednesday, 17 on Thursday, and 7 on Friday. What is the mean of the math problems he did per school day?

Kaitlin ran 3 miles on Sunday, 4 miles on Tuesday, 6 miles on Thursday, and 1 mile on Friday. She did not run on the remaining three days of the week. In that week, how many miles did she run on average per day?

Brain Box

We find the **mean** of a series of numbers by adding all the terms in the series together and then dividing the sum by the number of terms.

Statistics and Probability

Mean

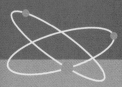

Outliers

Find the mean of each of these sets of numbers, rounding to the nearest whole number if necessary. Next, circle the outlier. Then find the mean of each set without the outlier.

4; 4; 5; 6; 8; 9; 27

mean: _____

outlier: _____

mean without outlier: _____

150; 165; 201; 350; 382; 800

mean: _____

outlier: _____

mean without outlier: _____

25; 1,056; 1,118; 1,245; 1,508

mean: _____

outlier: _____

mean without outlier: _____

Answer the questions.

Haley got 88, 92, 86, 94, and 95 on her math homework this month. But then she didn't turn one in, so she got a zero. What is her current mean score?

What would her mean score be if the zero were dropped from the record?

Brain Box

In statistics, an **outlier** is a number that varies a great deal from the other numbers in a set.

Statistics and Probability

Outliers

Find the Median

For each set, put the numbers in order and then circle the median.

1; 25; 26; 14; 13; 1; 4; 7; 9

_____

85; 75; 77; 96; 35; 101; 38; 40; 39; 42; 41

_____

25; 25; 36; 37; 28; 30; 31; 27; 28

_____

256; 105; 352; 289; 1,835

_____

Solve.

The ages of the kids at Jacob's party are 11, 11, 12, 12, 10, 12, 11, 13, 11, and 12. Jacob's mom is 42. What is the median age of all the people at Jacob's party?

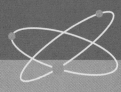

Brain Box

We find the **median** of a series of numbers by putting the terms in numerical order and then finding the number in the center.

If the set has an even number of terms, there will be two numbers in the center. The median is equal to the mean of those two numbers.

Statistics and Probability

Median

Pizza Parts

Use the data on the number of slices each student ate during February to answer the questions.

1, 2, 2, 2, 2, 3, 3, 3, 3, 3, 3, 4, 4, 4, 4, 5, 5, 5, 6, 7, 7, 8, 8

What is the median of this data set?

The 25th percentile is the number halfway between the median and the lowest number in the set.
What is that number?

The 75th percentile is the number halfway between the median and the highest number in the set.
What is that number?

What percentage of the data falls between these percentiles?

What is the interquartile range of this data?

Brain Box

The **interquartile range** describes the data in the middle of a data set—all the data that doesn't fall into the top quarter or the bottom quarter of the data.

We find it by subtracting the 75th percentile of the data from the 25th percentile.

Statistics and Probability

Interquartile range

Draw a box plot that displays the data on the previous page, including its interquartile ranges.

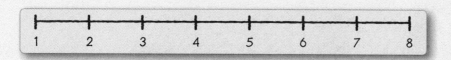

241

Brain Box

A box plot shows the variability of data by displaying its interquartile ranges—the 25th, 50th, and 75th percentiles.

The box plot is completed by lines that run along the number line from those boxes to the lowest and highest points in the data.

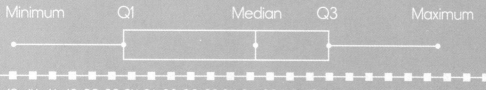

Statistics and Probability

Mean absolute deviation

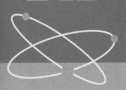

In or Out

Tell whether each item is a **measure of center** or a **measure of variability**.

median _____

mean _____

interquartile range _____

Brain Box

Interquartile range helps us understand data by dividing it into four equal ranges.

A **measure of center** helps us understand the center of the data better.

A **measure of variability** helps us understand how widely the data vary.

Mean absolute deviation tells us the absolute distance of any number in a set from the mean.

Social Studies

Social Studies

Around the World

Write the names of each of these countries in the appropriate place on the world map.

Canada Mexico France Germany India United Kingdom Italy Spain

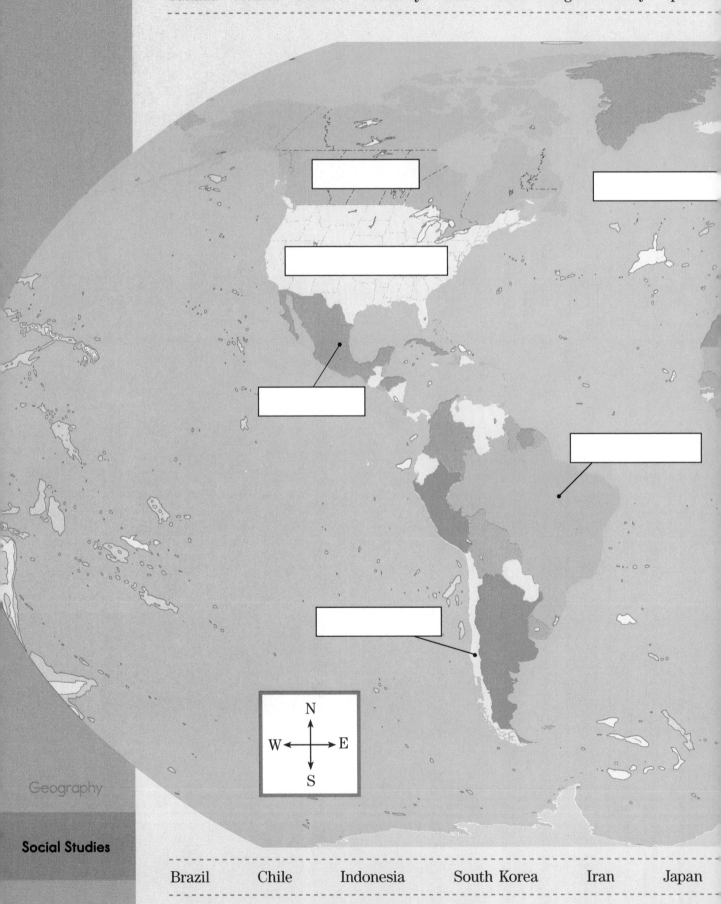

Geography

Brazil   Chile   Indonesia   South Korea   Iran   Japan

Norway   Russia   South Africa   Nigeria   Iraq   Afghanistan   Israel

Pakistan   China   Sweden   Australia   United States of America

Greek Democracy

Read Pericles's speech about his definition of democracy and why he believes democracy works. Then answer the questions that follow.

"Our constitution does not copy the laws of neighboring states. We are a pattern to others rather than imitators ourselves. Its administration favors the many instead of the few. This is why it is called a democracy. If we look to the laws, they afford equal justice to all in their private differences. If citizens do not have social standing, their advancement in public life comes from their reputation for capacity, because class considerations are not allowed to interfere with merit. Nor does poverty bar the way. If a man is able to serve the state, he is not hindered by the obscurity of his condition.

"The freedom which we enjoy in our government also extends to our ordinary life. There, instead of exercising jealous surveillance over each other, we do not feel called upon to be angry with our neighbor for doing what he likes, or even to indulge those injurious looks which cannot fail to be offensive, although they inflict no positive penalty.

"But all this ease in our private relations does not make us lawless as citizens. Against this, fear is our chief safeguard, teaching us to obey the magistrates and the laws, particularly those that protect the injured, whether those laws are actually on the statute book, or belong to that code which, although unwritten, cannot be broken without acknowledged disgrace."

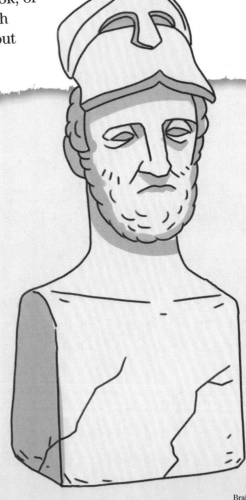

What does Pericles say is the definition of democracy?

_____

_____

According to Pericles, what two things do not keep an Athenian citizen from participating in society?

_____

_____

What does Pericles say is the chief safeguard against lawlessness in Athens?

_____

_____

What two kinds of laws does Pericles describe in the final paragraph?

_____

_____

What do you think was Pericles's purpose in giving this speech?

_____

_____

Brain Box

About 2,500 years ago, the world's first **democracies** arose in Greece. Pericles was a great Greek statesman, sometimes known as "the first citizen of Athens." He led Athens in the Peloponnesian War and also started the building projects that are now the many classical ruins that people still visit today, including the famous Parthenon.

Democracy

Social Studies

Echoes in History

Pericles said, "We are a pattern to others rather than imitators ourselves." Throughout history, many people have looked back at Greek democracy as a pattern for other democracies.

How do you think Pericles's ideas affect the world today?

_____
_____
_____
_____

In what ways is modern democracy similar to what Pericles describes? Name at least two similarities.

_____
_____

In what ways is modern democracy different from Greek democracy? Name at least two differences.

_____
_____

Historical patterns

Social Studies

Limited and Unlimited

Read the descriptions of different forms of government. Then decide whether they are limited or unlimited forms of government.

A country in which no decisions are made without the approval of religious leaders.

Limited	Unlimited

A country in which all officials are elected via voting by all citizens.

Limited	Unlimited

A city in which nothing can be done without the support of the mayor.

Limited	Unlimited

A country in which a small handful of people make decisions because they control the military.

Limited	Unlimited

A country in which people can vote to remove leaders if they are displeased with their leadership.

Limited	Unlimited

Brain Box

A **limited form** of government is one in which no one person or group has complete power.

An **unlimited form** of government is one in which one person or group has all the power.

Governments

Social Studies

Defining Democracy

Put these facts in order to better understand the history of democracy. Write the correct order in the spaces.

The 14th Amendment of the United States Constitution was ratified in 1868, granting freed slaves the full rights of citizenship—including the right to vote. But in many places, this right was difficult to exercise due to local restrictions.

The French Revolution began in 1789, signaling the start of a worldwide shift from traditions of monarchy to systems of democracy.

Although earlier forms of democracy may have existed around the world, the most influential early democracies arose among Greek city-states around 500 BCE. Instead of a single monarch, an elite group of men controlled the government. Women and slaves could not participate as citizens.

Democracy

Social Studies

○ In the present day, over half of the world's population lives under some form of electoral democracy.

○ America passed the Civil Rights Act of 1964, enforcing the right of all people, regardless of race, gender, or creed.

○ The United States ratified its Constitution in 1788, creating the first modern democracy. All American men had the right to vote for a representative government. Women and slaves did not have this right.

○ The 19th Amendment of the United States Constitution was ratified in 1920, giving American women the right to vote.

Democracy

Social Studies

Defining Democracy

Use the facts on the previous page to answer the questions below.

How long after the United States Constitution was ratified was the 14th Amendment ratified?

_____

_____

How long after the 14th Amendment was ratified did women receive the right to vote?

_____

_____

How long after the 14th Amendment was ratified did the Civil Rights Act guarantee voting rights for all Americans?

_____

_____

Who were the last group of people to receive the right to vote, according to the United States Constitution?

_____

_____

Starting from the date of the ratification of the Constitution, how many years did it take for democracy to become the most prevalent form of government in the world today?

_____

_____

Democracy

Social Studies

Reflections on Democracy

Democracy means we all have the right to state our own opinions.
What are your opinions about democracy?

If you could change one thing about the government today, what would it be?

What do you believe is the best thing about democracy?

Would you rather be a king or queen or be a president?

Would you rather live in a country headed by a king or queen or by a president?

Democracy

Social Studies

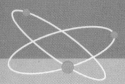

Rights and Limits

Read the lines below from the **Bill of Rights**. Then answer the questions about what limits each right puts on the government.

Bill of

Amendment I: Congress shall make no law respecting an establishment of religion, or prohibiting the free exercise thereof; or abridging the freedom of speech, or of the press; or the right of the people peaceably to assemble, and to petition the Government for a redress of grievances.

Amendment II: . . . The right of the people to keep and bear arms shall not be infringed.

Amendment IV: . . . The right of the people to be secure in their persons, houses, papers, and effects, against unreasonable searches and seizures shall not be violated. . . .

Amendment VI: In all criminal prosecutions, the accused shall enjoy the right to a speedy and public trial, by an impartial jury. . . .

Rights

According to the First Amendment, what six things may the government not make laws against?

_____   _____

_____   _____

_____   _____

According to the Second Amendment, what two things may the government not prevent its citizens from doing?

_____   _____

According to the Fourth Amendment, what two things may the government not do?

_____   _____

According to the Sixth Amendment, what three things must the government provide an accused person?

_____   _____

_____

Brain Box

The **Bill of Rights** refers to the first ten amendments to the United States Constitution.

Rights

Social Studies

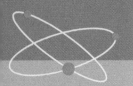

World Cities

Match each city with the country in which it is located by drawing arrows from the city to the country. Then identify each city on the map.

City	**Country**
Mexico City	Brazil
Berlin	Australia
Moscow	China
Shanghai	United States of America
New York City	Germany
Istanbul	Turkey
Sydney	Russia
Rio de Janeiro	Mexico

Geography

Social Studies

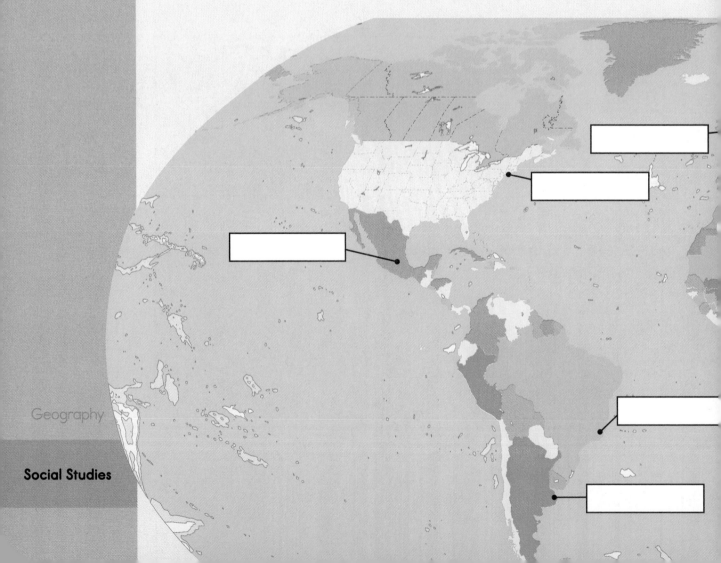

City

Rome

Beijing

Cairo

Paris

Cape Town

Jerusalem

London

Dubai

Tokyo

Jakarta

Seoul

Karachi

New Delhi

Buenos Aires

Country

United Kingdom

Argentina

Japan

Pakistan

India

Egypt

South Africa

Indonesia

South Korea

China

Italy

France

Israel

United Arab Emirates

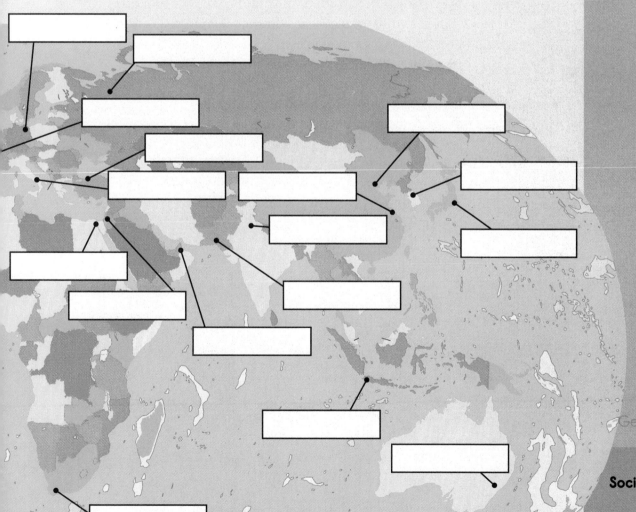

Different Perspectives

Read the two opinions below on the way humans affect the environment. Then answer the questions that follow.

Humans need to be more careful about how we treat the environment. Almost everywhere we go, you can find signs that we've been there. Those signs aren't always good. And one of the worst signs of human impact on the environment is a city. Our cities destroy miles and miles of wetlands and animal habitats. They belch pollution and produce all kinds of waste. We should go back to the days when everyone lived closer to the land—we were much more careful with everything we had.

—Ruris

Humans need to be more careful about how we treat the environment. And one way we can do that is by living in cities. When we live in cities, we don't take up as many resources, because we live in small apartments instead of big houses. We take public transportation instead of creating pollution by driving everywhere. Unlike in the suburbs, where only a few people will live with big lawns on acres of land, thousands and thousands of people can live in a single acre of a city. That means that city dwellers have less impact overall on the environment than people outside a city. Want to do something good for the environment? Move to a city.

—Urbis

Both essays begin with the same sentence. Do the two writers agree with each other?

_____

What is the main idea of Ruris's argument?

_____

_____

_____

_____

What is the main idea of Urbis's argument?

_____

_____

_____

_____

What points does Ruris seem to avoid?

_____

_____

_____

_____

What points does Urbis seem to avoid?

_____

_____

_____

_____

Perspectives

Social Studies

I Was There

Read the accounts below of people who were present on the first night a famous musician ever played. Then answer the questions on the following page.

Jesse: "These days people talk about it like it was a sold-out show at Carnegie Hall, but really it was a small club, and it was only half-full. Of course, I was there. I was always at all the best shows. I saw several other performers who are famous now before anyone else knew their name. So this wasn't such a big deal for me. But, yeah, I guess she played pretty well that night."

Sharon: "I mean, it was the middle of July. The city was half-empty, and so was Joe's. But she played a beautiful show. I remember she was wearing this very beautiful ring on her left hand, and it sparkled every time she strummed the guitar. I don't remember seeing Jesse there. I don't think he was."

A. J.: "To be honest, she wasn't that great yet. I mean, she's great now. But the reality is, the place was only half-full, and she was pretty nervous. She didn't really get comfortable until the last few songs. But then she knocked it out of the park. She did have this beautiful ring on her right hand. I remember once the flash from it left me blind for a second, so all I could hear was her voice."

What fact do all three sources agree on, besides the fact that the singer sang that night?

_____

_____

How do Sharon and A. J. contradict each other?

_____

_____

_____

How do Sharon and Jesse contradict each other?

_____

_____

_____

What does Jesse seem to be concerned with, besides telling the story?

_____

_____

_____

What does A. J. mention that no one else does?

_____

_____

_____

Brain Box

Primary sources are original documents and objects.

Secondary sources are interpretations that can be created by using primary and secondary sources.

Primary and secondary sources

Social Studies

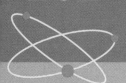

The Full Report

Read this passage about the first time a famous singer sang. Then compare it to the primary sources you read earlier to answer the questions.

On July 4, 1977, Vonda Peacock played her first-ever public show, at Joseph's Country Bar, on the Lower East Side in New York City. A respectable 77 tickets were sold that evening, during which time Peacock played standards as well as a few of her own compositions. She famously wore a blue velvet dress and her grandmother's sapphire ring. The performance signaled the advent of a major new star on the scene, and the world of music has never been the same.

List four facts that the secondary source includes in the first sentence that none of the primary sources mentions.

_____

_____

_____

_____

Why do you think none of the primary sources mentioned those facts?

_____

_____

All three sources who were at the show mention a fact that the writer of this article doesn't seem to know. What is that fact?

_____

How is the way Sharon refers to the name of the club different from the way this writer refers to it?

_____

_____

Read the last sentence of the article. Do you think all the people who attended the club that night would have agreed with the writer's statement?

_____

_____

_____

English and Empire

Use the maps and graphs to answer the questions.

British Empire

Is there any continent where the British Empire had no control?

_____

Over which continent did the British Empire have the largest percentage of control?

_____

What percent of that continent did the British Empire control?

_____

Over which continent did the British Empire have the second-largest percentage of control?

_____

Brain Box

The British Empire reached its height in the early 1900s.

The British Empire included one-fifth of the world's population and almost a quarter of the world's entire landmass.

Human migration

Social Studies

Copyright

Read the guidelines for the use of information.

Fair Use grants the limited use of copyrighted material in certain situations, especially if the use is not commercial, only uses a part of the original work, and transforms the original. Fair use may apply in criticism, commentary, and parody; reporting, education, and research; search engines and library archiving.

Creative Commons licenses allow an author to give up the copyright to a work for public use.

Open Source allows free, universal access to a product's design or blueprint.

Public Domain refers to works whose copyright has ended. In the United States, this usually occurs 70 years after the death of the author or 95 years after publication.

Brain Box

When in doubt, what should you do? Cite your source!

Now decide what you would do in the situations below.
Choose the guideline that you would follow.

You want to quote one paragraph of a book on the Wild West as part
of a research paper.

OK   Get Permission

Based on which guidelines: _____

You want to get a look at a computer code that is open to the public.
It's a free online operating system that was built by many different coders.

OK   Get Permission

Based on which guidelines: _____

You want to quote an article by an author who has voluntarily given
up the right to her work so that it can be used for free by the public.

OK   Get Permission

Based on which guidelines: _____

You love a poem published last year and want to distribute copies of it to
everyone in your class.

OK   Get Permission

Based on which guidelines: _____

You want to put on a play that was originally written in 1911.

OK   Get Permission

Based on which guidelines: _____

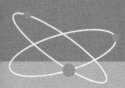

What Is the Internet?

Read the selection below. Then answer the questions that follow.

Many people spend a lot of time on the Internet. But what does that mean? Where do you go when you go "on the Internet"?

The things we look at on the Internet don't reside on our own computers or devices. Instead, they reside on a giant web of interconnected networks. So the Internet doesn't exist in any one place. It exists in many parts on billions of different computers around the world. All of these networks and devices are able to communicate with one another because they all use the same language, or Internet protocol suite, known as TCP/IP.

When you go to an address on the Internet, you create a connection between your device and one of those billions of other devices to receive the information another user has posted at that location—or to create and post your own information.

That means that anyone who wants to and has the equipment can create a brand-new part of the Internet and share it with the world.

Brain Box

The **Internet** began in the late 1960s and early 1970s as a way for scientists to exchange information with each other.

Information technology

Social Studies

How many computers and devices are a part of the Internet?

_____

What allows all electronic devices to communicate?

_____

_____

What happens when you go to an "address" on the Internet?

_____

_____

_____

Who can create content for the Internet?

_____

_____

Computer Components

Match these computer components with their function.

case

monitor

battery

motherboard

Central Processing Unit (CPU)

Random Access Memory (RAM)

a visual display

integrated circuitry
that connects components

protective shell that contains
most other components

performs most calculations

stores information that
is in current use by CPU

supplies energy
without a power cord

Science

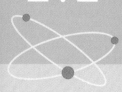

Basic Building Blocks

Read this description of the basic building blocks of **matter**.

Brain Box

What is matter made of? Everything in the world is made from particles so tiny you could never see them with the human eye.

Proton: a subatomic particle (a particle that's smaller than an atom) with a positive charge, at the nucleus of an atom.

Neutron: a subatomic particle without an electric charge, at the nucleus of an atom.

Electron: a particle with a negative charge, that orbits the nucleus of an atom.

Atom: a core of protons and neutrons orbited by electrons.

Nucleus: the center of an atom that is made up of protons and neutrons

Physics

Science

Label these parts of an atom. Then answer the questions.

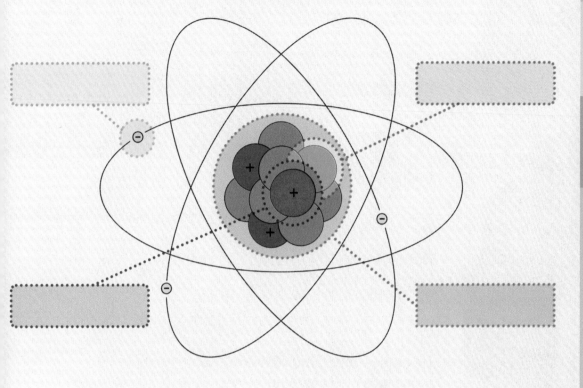

What is bigger, a neutron or an atom? _____

What is the smallest part of an atom? _____

Which of these are not found in the nucleus of an atom:
proton, electron, or neutron? _____

Brain Box

Atoms are mostly empty space. Pretend an atom is the size of a large city. In that case, each **proton** and **neutron** would be about the size of one person. But each **electron** would only be about the size of a freckle on your arm!

Physics

Science

Renewable or Not?

Read each sentence. Which resource is **renewable**? Which is **nonrenewable**? Write your answer on the line.

River water used to generate hydroelectricity through a dam

_____

Coal mined from ancient deposits

_____

Hardwood from old-growth forests that grew over the course of centuries

_____

Drinking water pumped up from aquifers that took thousands of years to fill

_____

Lumber from responsibly forested pine

_____

Solar power collected in cells charged by the sun

_____

Brain Box

A **renewable resource** is one that can be replenished after it is used.
A **nonrenewable resource** is one that cannot be replenished.

Where Is the Water?

Put these elements of the **water cycle** in order.

STEP _____

Water evaporating from the surface of the oceans and the land condenses, causing clouds to form.

STEP _____

Water evaporates from the surface of the ocean and the surface of the land.

STEP _____

The runoff of precipitation flows back into the lakes, rivers, and oceans.

STEP _____

Full of condensed water, clouds rain down on the land, lakes, rivers, and oceans.

Water cycle

The World's Water

Identify the following **bodies of water** on the world map.

- ◯ Pacific Ocean
- ◯ Atlantic Ocean
- ◯ Amazon River
- ◯ Mississippi River
- ◯ Mediterranean Sea
- ◯ Indian Ocean
- ◯ Arctic Ocean
- ◯ Southern Ocean

Brain Box

About 71 percent of the world's surface is covered with water.

Almost all of that water (about 96.5 percent) is in the oceans.

That means that all the rivers, lakes, underground reservoirs, and ice in the world contain less than 5 percent of the world's water.

Oceanography

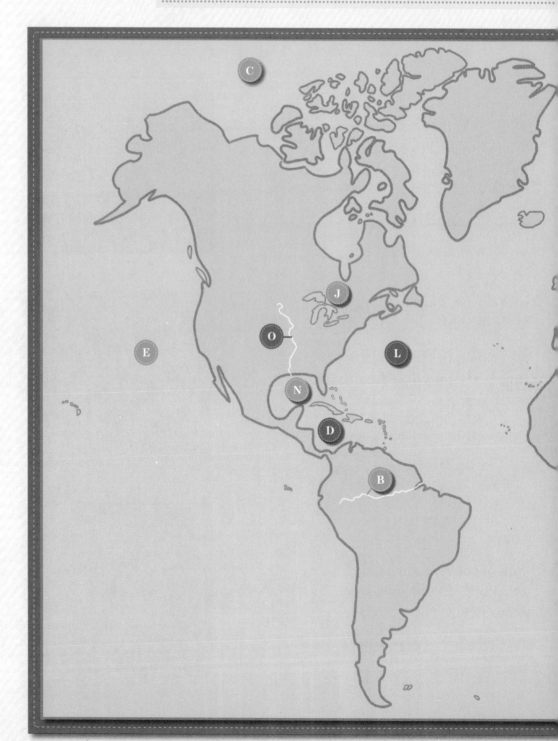

○ Great Lakes
○ South China Sea
○ Yangtze River
○ Danube River

○ Ganges River
○ Zambezi River
○ Volga River
○ Caspian Sea

○ Gulf of Mexico
○ Bering Sea
○ Caribbean Sea
○ Nile River

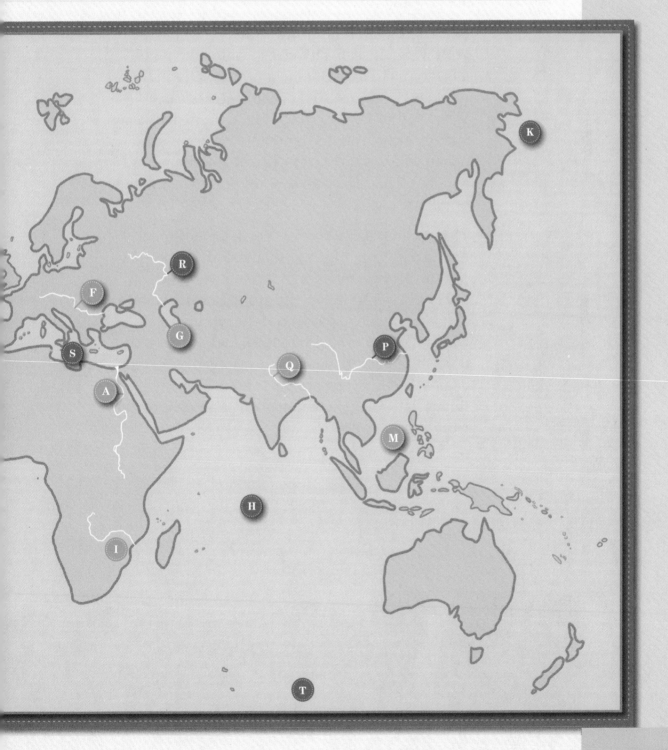

Science

Finding Fresh Water

Read about the world's supply of fresh water. Then answer the questions that follow.

Fresh water is a foundation of all life. Most life forms, both plant and animal, are composed largely of water. Humans, for instance, are made up of about half water. So we need fresh water to survive and thrive.

Because most of the world's surface is covered with water, it seems like fresh water should be easy for us to find. But most of the water in the world is in oceans. And ocean water is salty. Why? For millions of years, rain has carried salt and minerals from the land into the oceans. So ocean water is no longer drinkable for humans, and isn't a good source of water for most animals or plants.

That means that all life on Earth is dependent on the 5 percent of water that isn't in the world's oceans. In fact, most of that fresh water is either buried far below the ground or frozen into glaciers. About 30 percent of the world's fresh water is considered groundwater, and almost 69 percent is ice in glaciers. That means that all the clouds, lakes, rivers, certain swamps, and living things in the world contain about 1 percent of the world's fresh water.

Water cycle

How much of the water in the world is fresh water?

_____

What percent of the fresh water in the world is on the surface,
in the form of rivers, lakes, and some swamps?

_____

Where is most of the fresh water in the world found?

_____

_____

Why is the ocean salty?

_____

_____

_____

_____

About how much of a human is made up of water?

_____

Waves, Currents, and Tides

Read about the ocean in motion. Then answer the questions that follow.

The ocean is full of motion. When you enjoy a day at the beach, you see it all. Big waves come crashing onto the shore. Swimmers need to be careful of small hidden currents. Big boats go by on the horizon, following the giant currents that run through the entire ocean. And every few hours the tide goes out, and then comes back in.

What causes all this motion? The wind you feel on your face at the beach causes many of the waves—anything from a small ripple to a big swell. But waves can be caused by other things. You can create a wave in a bathtub by dropping a toy, or kicking your feet, and the same is true in the ocean. Underwater earthquakes and disturbances at the shore, such as landslides, can also cause waves.

Many people know the feeling of a current tugging them at the shore. Those small currents are caused when different types of waves break on the beach. There are also giant currents that carry water all around the world and affect weather patterns. These large worldwide currents are formed in part by wind on the surface of the ocean. They're affected by the rotation of the Earth—and by the shape of the shore the water washes up against. Currents are also caused by the differences in the temperature and saltiness of water. When ice freezes at the poles of the Earth, cold, salty water is left. That water is denser than the rest of the water in the ocean, so it sinks. As it does, it displaces warmer water, and a current is created.

Through it all, the tides continue to come in and go out. They're not driven by big gusts of wind, or by temperature variations. Instead, tides respond to the gravitational pull of the sun and the moon. And because the relationship of the sun and the moon to Earth changes, tides also change.

In fact, the sun provides most of the energy that drives the motion of the ocean. It's the presence or the absence of the sun that creates the wind that drives waves. It's the heat of the sun that causes polar ice to melt or form and thus creates currents. And it's the pull of both the sun and the moon that causes tides.

So when you sit on the beach, enjoying the water and the sun, you also get a taste of the massive forces that move the whole ocean.

What five factors contribute to large and small currents?

What two things beyond Earth cause the tides?

What three factors create waves?

What is left behind after polar ice forms?

What provides most of the energy for motion in the ocean?

Building Blocks of Life

Match each part of a cell to the function it performs.

cell membrane

nuclear membrane

cytoplasm

nucleus

endoplasmic reticulum

golgi body

mitochondria

chloroplasts

lysosomes

chromatin

ribosomes

directs a cell's activities

the outer covering of a cell

large structure that contains chlorophyll in plants

creates energy and performs respiration

contains RNA and binds RNA together to synthesize proteins

a membrane network that makes, changes, and transports cellular materials mostly for use inside the cell

the covering of the nucleus

packages, strengthens, and protects DNA, and controls gene expression

the fluid inside a cell

makes, stores, and transports materials mostly for use outside the cell

contains enzymes that digest particles

Label these elements of the cell on the diagram below.

cell membrane

nucleus

endoplasmic reticulum

cytoplasm

nuclear membrane

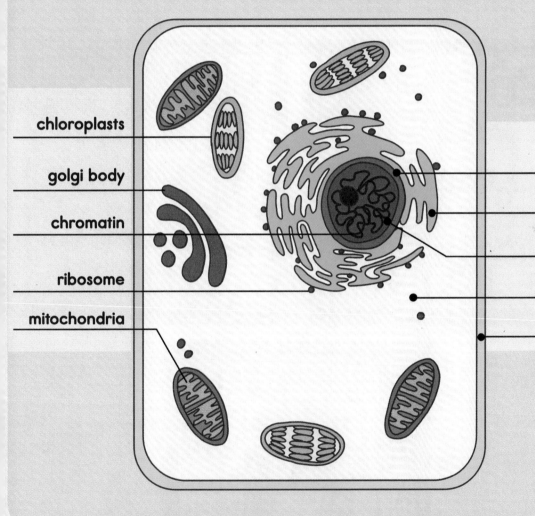

chloroplasts

golgi body

chromatin

ribosome

mitochondria

Bonus: Do you think this a plant or an animal cell? Why?

_____

Cell organization

Science

Atomic Numbers

Gather information from these entries on the **periodic table** to answer questions about these elements on the next page.

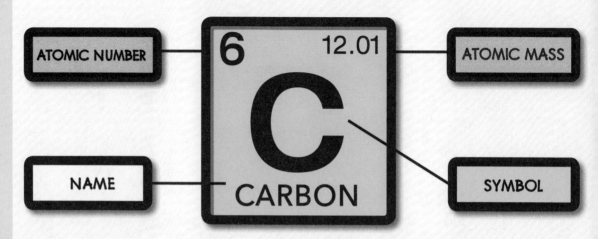

ATOMIC NUMBER

ATOMIC MASS

6   12.01

C

CARBON

NAME

SYMBOL

Brain Box

The **atomic number** of every element is also the number of protons in the nucleus of each atom of that element. Carbon's atomic number is 6. That means there are 6 protons in the nucleus of every carbon atom.

26   55.85

Fe

IRON

8   15.99

O

OXYGEN

1   1.01

H

HYDROGEN

Periodic table

Science

6	12.01
C	
CARBON	

26	55.85
Fe	
IRON	

8	15.99
O	
OXYGEN	

1	1.01
H	
HYDROGEN	

What element does the symbol O stand for?

_____

What is the symbol for iron?

_____

How many protons are there in an oxygen atom?

_____

How many more protons are there in an oxygen atom
than a hydrogen atom?

_____

How many more protons are there in an atom of iron
than in an atom of oxygen?

_____

Approximately how much more mass does oxygen have than
hydrogen?

_____

Periodic table

Science

What's the Temperature?

Read these different thermometers to answer the questions that follow.

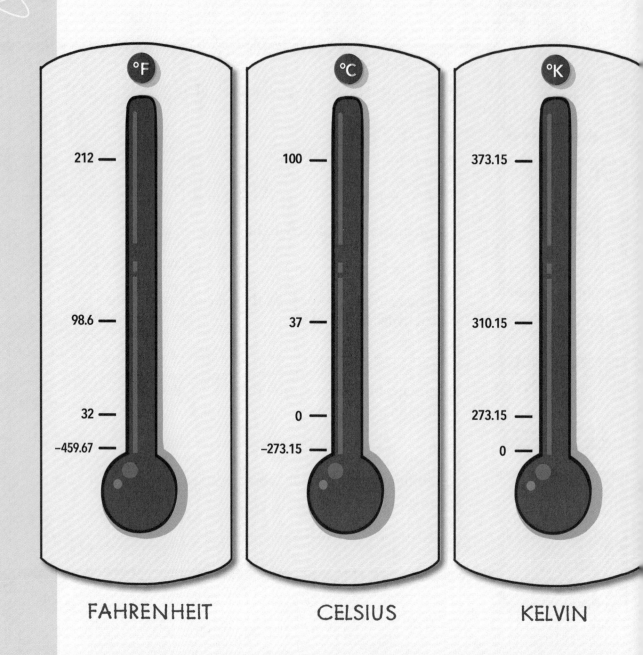

°F

212 —

98.6 —

32 —

−459.67 —

FAHRENHEIT

°C

100 —

37 —

0 —

−273.15 —

CELSIUS

°K

373.15 —

310.15 —

273.15 —

0 —

KELVIN

Brain Box

The **Kelvin scale** shows 0 at absolute zero, a temperature at which no heat energy remains.

The **Celsius scale** shows 0 at the freezing point of water.

Tradition has it that on the **Fahrenheit scale**, zero was the lowest temperature that the scientist Daniel Gabriel Fahrenheit could measure, and 100 was close to his own body temperature.

Scales

Science

The boiling point of water is 373.15°K. What is the boiling point of water on the Celsius scale?

The freezing point of water is 0°C. What is the freezing point of water on the Fahrenheit scale?

How many degrees is the freezing point of water away from the boiling point of water on the Fahrenheit scale?

How many degrees is the freezing point of water away from the boiling point of water on the Celsius scale?

Which is warmer, 273.15°K or 98.6°F?

Which is colder, 32°C or 32°F?

100°K

100°F

100°C

Kinetic or Potential

Read each description below. Decide whether each one is an example of **kinetic energy**, **potential energy**, or both.

a rock perched on the top of a mountain

a bicycle tire in motion

a meteor hurtling through space

a coiled spring

a ball swinging at the end of a string

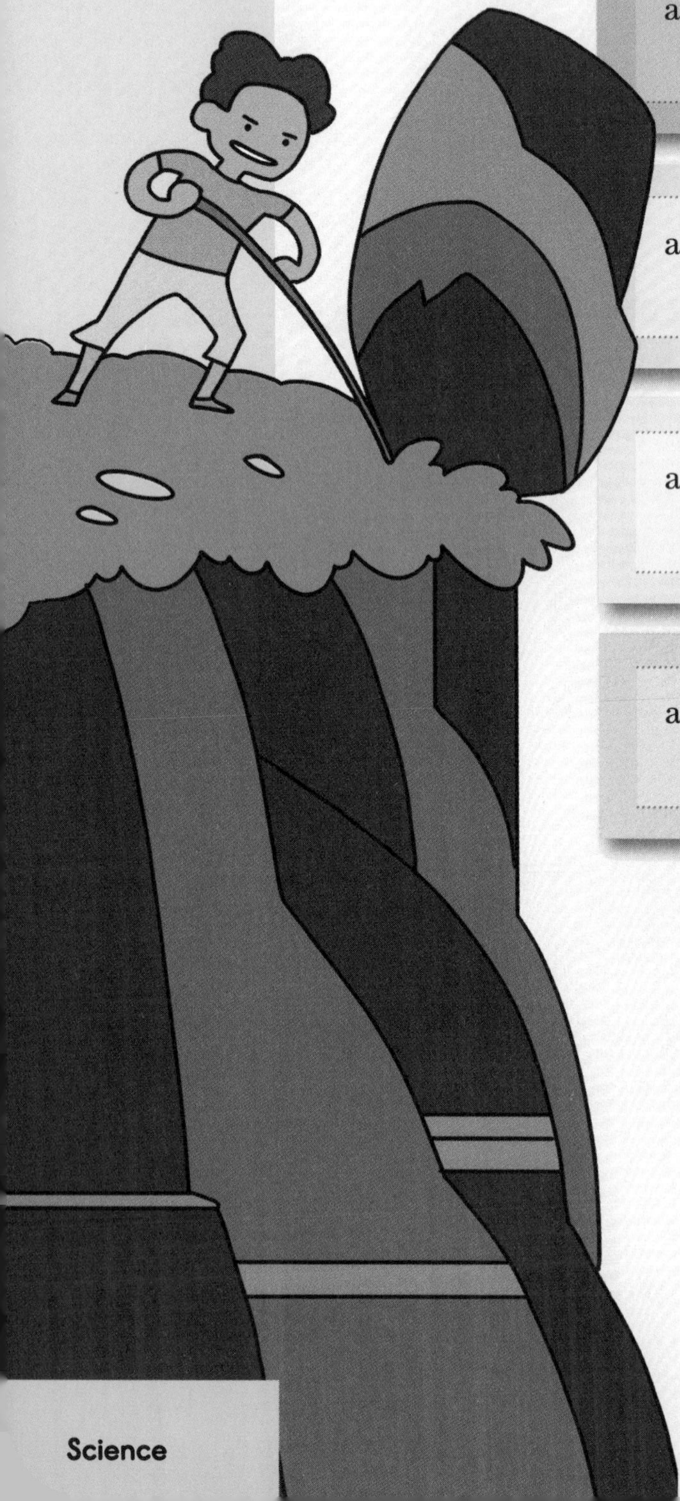

Brain Box

Kinetic energy is the energy an object possesses due to its motion.

Potential energy is energy stored by an object due to its position—where it is in relation to its surroundings.

Order of Operations

Put these steps of the **scientific method** in correct order.

Hypothesis: Based on your observations, come up with a possible but unproven answer to your question. ☐

Analyze: Analyze the data from your experiment. ☐

Accept or Reject Hypothesis: Decide whether, based on the data from your experiment, your hypothesis is correct or incorrect. ☐

Experiment: Design a procedure to test your hypothesis. ☐

Observation: Notice something interesting or seemingly unusual about the world. ☐

Science

You're the Scientist

Now design your own experiment.

What do you notice that is interesting about the world?
What things do you see that you wonder about?

_____

_____

What question would you like an answer to?

_____

Based on what you already know about the world, what do
you guess the answer to your question might be?

_____

_____

Design an experiment to test your hypothesis. What would
you need to do to find out the answer to your question?

_____

_____

_____

_____

Brain Box

Is an experiment successful when it proves your hypothesis? Yes! But an experiment is also successful when it disproves your hypothesis. It doesn't matter whether an experiment confirms what you believed to begin with or not. Any experiment that provides a clear answer is a success.

Scientific method

Science

If it's possible to conduct your experiment, record the data here. If not, manufacture some data. What do you think might happen if you ran the experiment? Record it here.

_____

_____

_____

_____

_____

_____

_____

_____

_____

_____

_____

_____

_____

_____

_____

_____

_____

_____

_____

You're the Scientist

What does your data seem to say about your hypothesis? Does it support it or not? Why or why not?

_____

_____

_____

Based on your experiment and data, do you believe your hypothesis is correct?

_____

What did you learn from the experiment? Did you learn anything you didn't expect to learn?

_____

_____

_____

Answer Key

(For pages not included in this section,
answers will vary.)

page 6

Soft G | **Hard G**

Soft G	Hard G
Genevieve	gumdrops
jawbreakers	Gus
just	gum
Jerry	nougat
jars	gooey
judge	grinned
giant	green
	grapes
	great
	good

page 7

assistance
attendance
disappearance
performance
difference
persistence

BONUS: disobedience

page 8

allowed / aloud	rain / reign
they're / there	waste / waist
writes / rights	sail / sale
days / daze	hour / our

page 9

forgetting	scarred
wondering	boosted
fitting	mapped
admitting	jumped
knitting	fanned
plotting	slipped
listening	played
excelling	crunched

page 10

pro	de
de	pro
pro	de
de	de
pro	pro

page 11

in	in
il	im
ir	in
im	il
in	in
im	ir
il	in
im	im

page 12

economic, atmosphere,
circumference, parallel,
encyclopedia, individual, metaphor,
virus, archaeologist, boundary

page 13

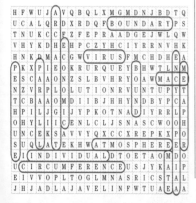

Bonus: penthouse, bound, mace, mate

page 14

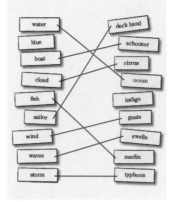

page 16

Answers may vary.

Facts

Paul Revere rode at midnight, on April 18.

Paul Revere had a friend.

The writer is writing from a time long after that date.

The British were enemies of Paul Revere and the local people.

No one was sure if the British would arrive by land or sea.

Paul Revere left instructions to hang signal lights in a church tower: one if the British were coming by land, and two if the British were coming by sea.

Paul Revere planned to spread the word throughout Middlesex so the people could arm themselves.

Inferences

Because the American Revolution started in 1775, "Seventy-five" probably refers to 1775.

This incident was probably part of a larger conflict.

Because Longfellow chose to write a poem about the event and the poem is still being read today, this is probably a major historical event.

page 18

work

Ben teases Tom about the fact that he has to "work." Tom stumps Ben with a question about the meaning of "work." The boys discuss the question of whether or not work can be fun.

Most people don't think work can be fun, but the line between work and fun is not always clear. What is and is not work can be a matter of perspective.

page 20

Answers may vary.

TOM

Tom is whitewashing a fence.
Tom notices Ben beside him, but he sticks to his work.
Tom's mouth waters for the apple.
Tom questions, "What is work?"
Tom says he likes painting the fence.

BEN

Ben was on his way to go swimming.
Ben stops to watch Tom paint.
Ben is eating an apple.
Ben becomes more interested in painting.
Ben asks if he can whitewash a little.

TOM

Tom does not let teasing bother him.
Tom likes apples.
Tom has a good imagination.
Tom is clever.
Tom is persuasive.

BEN

Ben likes to tease Tom.
Ben likes swimming.
Ben does not like to work.
Ben is convinced by Tom's argument.
Ben eventually thinks whitewashing could be fun.

Ben changes during the course of the conversation. At first, he thinks of whitewashing as work. By the end, he thinks it might be something he likes to do.

page 21

Tom is whitewashing the fence.
Tom brushes the fence artfully.
Tom and Ben discuss whether painting the fence is work. Tom begins carefully painting the fence again. Ben asks if he can whitewash the fence.

"Artist," "gentle sweep," "work," "daintily," etc. The theme "What is work?" reoccurs.

The language makes the reader wonder whether or not painting the fence is work.

Ben thinks the fence represents work.

Tom thinks the fence could represent fun if you think and act like an artist.

Instead of working quickly, Tom takes his time and paints carefully—like an artist.

Tom has a strong imagination.

Yes, the fence changes from a chore to a chance to paint.

The fence stands for a person's perspective—if you change your perspective on something, it could change from work to play.

page 23

The characters expected to eat breakfast. Their expectations change when they are told about a family in need and decide to give their breakfast to the family.

Amy chooses to offer the food that she likes the most. This shows that Amy is generous.

Jo makes decisions quickly, and she is selfless.

Jo is usually seen as a troublemaker.

The characters get bread and milk instead of an extravagant breakfast. They also got the chance to make another family happy instead of making themselves happy.

The different experience shows the characters that giving to the needy can be more fulfilling than keeping things for yourself.

page 33

Answers may vary.

1) The narrator is the son of the owner of the Admiral Benbow inn. 2) He lives at the inn. 3) He is older now than he was at the time of the story. 4) He knows how to read and write. 5) He spends time with his father at the inn.

1) The guest has brown skin; 2) has a sabre cut; 3) walks slowly; 4) has a sea chest; 5) is tall and strong.

The narrator does not seem to like the way the guest is dressed; details: 1) He describes the guest's clothes as "dirty" and "soiled." 2) The narrator does not seem to like the way the guest talks. He describes his speech as "rough." 3) The narrator is impressed by the way the guest drinks rum, "like a connoisseur."

The narrator is interested in the guest's clothing, in the way the guest speaks, and in the way he carries himself. But the narrator also notes that the guest seems to have more dignity than his clothing. We can learn that the narrator is naturally curious, that he believes you can learn something about people from the way that they are dressed, but that he knows there is more to a person than just their outward appearance.

page 34

Answers may vary.

The innkeeper wishes he had more guests.

The guest is glad to hear that the inn doesn't have many guests.

The innkeeper would make more money if he had more guests.

The guest may enjoy solitude, or

e may be trying to avoid meeting
people he doesn't like or with
whom he is afraid to cross paths.

page 35

Answers may vary.

1) The narrator uses a formal
adult vocabulary in setting the
scene. 2) The narrator states that
all these things happened years
ago. 3) The narrator mentions his
adult acquaintances like Squire
Trelawney and Dr. Livesey, who
asked him to write about Treasure
Island.

1) The narrator takes no part in the
story, but only observes while his
father takes action. 2) The narrator
describes the guest without making
any comparisons that are beyond
the scope of the world he knew as
a child. 3) The narrator states that
these things happened years ago.

The narrator may have been
impressed with the way the guest
drank his rum when he was
younger, but it is unlikely he knew
the world "connoisseur" as a child.

The description of the guest as a
"brown old seaman with the sabre
cut" uses a child's simple language.

The description of the guest
that begins "a tall, strong, heavy,
nut-brown man" displays an
adult's organization, detail, and
complexity.

page 39

Answers may vary.

Time of day: Early morning

Location: a pine forest, or woods,
not far from Weybridge

Description: a huge cylinder,
diameter of about thirty yards,
large and uneven shape, too hot to
approach closely or touch, a black
mark on one side of the cylinder.

Events: An object was found buried
in the sand. It was surrounded by a
tree that had been destroyed. The
narrator approached the object. It
was hot. The narrator was alone.
Ash began to fall from the cylinder.
A noise came from inside. The top
began to rotate very slowly.

page 41

1) A tree was destroyed by the
spaceship. b) *Shivered* gives a
sense of fear.

2) The cylinder was too hot to
touch. b) *Forbid* gives a sense of
danger or wrongdoing.

3) Something was falling off the
spaceship. b) *Raining* gives a
sense of a steady patter.

4) When a piece fell off, the man
was frightened. b) The phrase
"brought his heart into his mouth"
gives a sense that the man is
extremely scared.

pages 46–47

Answers may vary.

a) cold, hard, imperious
b) Mary has never had friends
before or played with anyone. Even
her ayah didn't like her. So it is a
big event for her to connect with
another person—or even a bird.

a) soft, eager, coaxing
b) Mary is less guarded at the end.
Her tone of voice is softer.

Ben's comments make Mary feel
slightly uncomfortable.

She has never been treated or
spoken to in an honest way. Her
conversation with Ben makes her
think about her life in a different
way.

Mary realizes that she is lonely.

Ben's comment that the bird is
lonely, and Ben telling her that she
is just like him.

The bird decides to be her friend.

Ben

page 52

Answers may vary.

1) I'd study the effect of sunlight
on bacteria. 2) I'd study the new
bacterium.

1) I'd study the poet's interest
in recipes. 2) I'd study her
relationship with the other famous
poet.

page 53

Answers may vary.

obnoxious, suspected, unpopular

happy, remarkable, silent, prompt,
frank, explicit, decisive

1) Adams gets the second-highest
number of votes of any committee
member. 2) Adams is able to get
other people to vote for Jefferson.
3) Adams is able to convince
Jefferson to do what Adams thinks
is best.

1) Jefferson is already known
as a writer. 2) He allows his
writing to be passed around the
Congress. 3) He does not refuse the
appointment to write the draft with
Adams. 4) Adams gives him a list
of reasons why he should write the
draft, but Jefferson does not give
Adams a list of reasons why Adams
should write it.

page 54

Facts are underlined; opinions are
circled.

Mr. Jefferson came into Congress,
in June 1775, and brought with him
a reputation for literature, science,
and a happy talent of composition.
Writings of his were handed
about, remarkable for the peculiar
felicity of expression. Though a
silent member in Congress, he was

so prompt, frank, explicit, and
decisive upon committees and in
conversation, not even Samuel
Adams was more so, that he soon
seized upon my heart; and upon
this occasion I gave him my vote,
and did all in my power to procure
the votes of others. I think he had
one more vote than any other,
and that placed him at the head
of the committee. I had the next
highest number, and that placed
me second. The committee met,
discussed the subject, and then
appointed Mr. Jefferson and me
to make the draught. I suppose
because we were the two first on
the list.

page 55

Answers may vary.

He came to Congress in June 1775.

He is knowledgable in literature
and science, and he is a talented
writer.

prompt, frank, explicit, decisive

Yes; he was a silent member
of Congress, but he spoke well
in committees and in personal
conversations.

page 56

paraphrase
plagiarism
paraphrase
plagiarism
plagiarism
paraphrase
paraphrase

page 57

Answers may vary.

Mom probably left the pie on the
table. There's no reason to believe
she'd leave a note if there wasn't
really a pie.

Your sister probably ate only
one piece, or maybe a bit more.
Otherwise, there wouldn't have
been anything left for the dog to
have on his nose.

The dog used the chair to climb up
on the table and eat the pie. He was
caught in the act and has evidence
on his nose.

Mom is likely the most credible,
because she has no reason to lie.

The dog is the least credible,
because the evidence contradicts
his claim not to have done anything
wrong.

page 58

Answers may vary.

escape
being poor
submerged
thorough, strict
comforted
uniform, boring
variety

page 59

James Smith, 1918

1925

because they'd had three children
in the past several years

Jimmy and Agnes Smith, 1947

Jimmy was Tina and James's son.

They moved to Florida.

page 60

No.

She doesn't want to go to the drive-
through.

bad weather, stuck in the car,
they're out of everything, Danny
Thompson works there

The family can sit down together
and eat healthier food.

Danny Thompson is there.

page 61

Trucker, Harry. Beards and
Blacktop. New York, NY: Evanston
Classics, 1967.

Peace, Warren. Battles Through the
Ages. Philadelphia, PA: Columbia
Publishing, 1951.

Day, Holly. Festive Celebrations,
from A to Z. Anchorage, AK:
Pendleton Books, 1989.

Cantfly, I. Falling from the Sky.
Deep Springs, CO: Aviatics Press,
1976.

page 62

Answers may vary.

mysterious wandering lab beakers,
careless lab assistants

Albert's carelessness

disorganized, distracted

thoughtful, careful, rational

page 63

Answers may vary.

Things are never where he put
them; he would never confuse
the vials.

She's seen Albert mix things up;
she's tried to help him before; he
may have a history of blowing
things up.

No. There are many other
possibilities, including the fact that
he might have something to do
with it.

Yes. All her evidence points
logically to Albert.

page 65

Answers may vary.

learning how to read

1) carries a book everywhere;
2) finishes his errands quickly;
3) carries bread as a bribe

slavery / freedom

". . . it is almost an unpardonable
offence to teach slaves to read in
this Christian country."

in the fact that Douglass is not allowed to read

page 66

Answers may vary.

to learn how to read

discontentment, a curse rather than a blessing

He is not allowed to read because he is not free.

He becomes even more aware that he is not free.

He sees and thinks about freedom everywhere, and in everything.

page 67

Answers may vary.

It is valuable, because he goes to a lot of trouble and risk to learn. But it can also lead to disturbing thoughts.

He thinks they are generous to help him, and that they believe he should have freedom.

little, white, kindly

He thinks it is unfair.

heavily upon my heart, torment and sting my soul to unutterable anguish, wretched condition, horrible pit, agony

page 68

Answers may vary.

when he says he wishes to be as free as the other boys when he grows up

The other boys are troubled that he will not grow up to be free like them.

He asks why he does not have the same rights they do. They hope one day he will.

sounds, things, seeing, hearing, feeling, stars, calm, wind, and storm

Freedom is the most important thing in the world to Douglass, and he can't escape his thoughts of freedom, no matter where he turns.

page 69

Answers may vary.

a sworn statement of facts

a doctor who specializes in the ears, nose, and throat

a place where a computer temporarily stores information

a slab of concrete that helps support structural elements in construction

a container for storing small amounts of liquid

page 70

Everybody knows ducks are the best animals in the world. The scientific name for the duck family is *Anatidae*. It's a beautiful name. Female ducks are called "hens" or "ducks." Male ducks are called

"drakes." And baby ducks are called "ducklings." There isn't anything cuter in the world than a duckling. And speaking of the world, there are ducks all over the world—except for Antarctica. Their webbed feet would probably get pretty cold on all that snow, because they don't have any fur to cover them. The ducks are covered with down, which mother ducks use to create a soft nest for their children. Ducks aren't fussy eaters, either. They're omnivores, which means they eat everything from grass to insects to fruit and fish. Ducks were domesticated as farm animals and pets over 500 years ago. All the domestic ducks in the world are descended from two kinds of ducks: either a mallard or a Muscovy. But today, there are many more domestic breeds of ducks—over 40. Ducks have always been my favorite kind of animal, and I hope now they're yours, too.

page 74

Answers may vary.

May I please have that?

I don't really enjoy doing this exercise.

I don't understand this. Can you help me?

When do you think we might be finished with this?

Would you like this?

I like that.

page 75

Answers may vary.

This is awesome!

Pass the butter, please.

Do you want to go to the store?

Let's go.

What are you talking about?

Thanks!

page 76

Many people believe that Socrates was the greatest philosopher who ever lived. In fact, some consider him to be the father of all philosophy. Philosophy is about the meaning of life and that kind of stuff. Socrates lived in Greece, in the fifth century BCE. I guess people kind of studied philosophy before him, but he really made it into a big deal. Philosophy used to be just for eggheads who wanted to sit around and talk about ideas. But Socrates had a different method of teaching. He didn't instruct his students on what to think. Instead, he asked them questions about what they thought, and helped them arrive at the answers themselves. Socrates was also interested in the practical implications of philosophy: how

it applied to regular people in day-to-day life. And that interest in the consequences of philosophy may have been Socrates's downfall. Eventually, he got himself killed by talking too much about what philosophy had to do with politics. But he had the last laugh. Because they couldn't kill his ideas. So everybody still has to read him today, two thousand five hundred years later.

page 80

However
Furthermore
For example
On the other hand
In conclusion

page 81

First
Next
Meanwhile
Finally

page 92

English:
pen
my report
book of poems

Physical Education:
sneakers
sports jersey
baseball bat

Science:
beaker
my report
lab notes
pen

page 95

3	The witness box exploded in a shower of white sparks and blue smoke.
1	As the guilty magician took the stand, he fastened a wad of exploding gum to his chair in the witness box.
6	But when the court finally came to order again, the magician had vanished.
4	The whole court erupted into chaos.
2	When the questioning became uncomfortable, the magician struck a match to the exploding gum.
5	The judge pounded her gavel and called for order.

page 96

The Smallville Litter Pickup had a small core of volunteers. But when Janice began to bring her famous chocolate chip cookies, word of the delicious snacks soon spread, and the number of volunteers almost quadrupled.

page 100

Answers may vary.

In June each year, the NBA (National Basketball Association) holds a draft to add new members to the league. Both international and U.S. college players are considered. College players who have already played 4 years of college basketball are automatically eligible for the

draft. Others have to declare their eligibility. A lottery determines which teams get to pick first. During the course of two rounds, different teams pick the players they think will play best. In the end, only 60 players are selected from the entire world. They're the newest members of the NBA.

page 102

He
They
them
her
His
their

page 103

Subjective:
he
they
she
we

Objective:
them
us
her
him

Possessive:
our
hers
their
his

Bonus question: her

page 104

I arrived on the scene just after 10:30 pm. The entire family was standing in the yard. Mr. Smith reported that he saw a strange shadow in the living room. Bobby, the son, claimed he heard weird noises sometime before his dad. He reported it to Mrs. Smith, who told him to go back to bed. My investigation led me to the living room, where I followed the noises and discovered Pete, the family dog. He was curled up beside a lamp that had fallen from a nearby table. As I approached, I saw another small furry object near the lightbulb: A tiny kitten Pete was keeping warm. I carried it outside, and introduced the newest member to the rest of the family.

page 105

I'm having a great time here at camp. I'm learning how to ride a horse this week. My favorite horse is a mare named Sparkplug. She is the fastest horse in the stables. She can't run for as long as the other horses, but she can beat them all in a short race. She can also jump like a champ. She is fast, but she is gentle. She is actually very patient with me. Even though she can run faster than any of the other horses, when she knows she has a new rider on her back, she won't ry to go too fast. But I'm getting comfortable enough now that I can trot and even canter without feeling too scared. And one day soon I'll get to take her out and actually feel what it's like when she gallops. I can't wait!

page 106
himself
yourselves
myself
ourselves
yourself
itself
herself
themselves

page 107
reflexive
intensive
reflexive
reflexive
intensive
reflexive
reflexive
intensive

page 109
You rushed down the stairs, but the train pulled away before you reached the platform.

I have a beautiful voice, and it's a pleasure to hear.

She wished it hadn't rained today, so that the game hadn't been canceled.

They were delighted to discover a candy bar at the bottom of the bag when they finished unpacking the groceries.

We discovered a new path in the woods and followed it until we found a hidden stream.

page 110
agrees
was
has
knows
has
is
minds
is

page 111
you ——▶ we
you ——▶ he
you ——▶ I
they ——▶ you
you ——▶ we
we ——▶ you
you ——▶ we

page 112
him
she
their
his
her
they
him

page 113
They
they
They
you
it
they
you

page 114
They say there's nothing like a bird's-eye view. But you have a hard time getting a bird's-eye view if you don't have wings—unless you go up in a hot-air balloon like I did last weekend. My dad and brother were with me, and he loved it! Everywhere you looked, it was a beautiful view. We saw an airplane. And a bird landed right on the edge of the balloon's basket. When we came down, they even let us wave to some of the people in the fields below. I just wanted to stay until the next time the balloon went back up, but my dad said we had to go. But as my dad helped my brother out of the basket, he said it wouldn't be the last time we got to go for a balloon ride.

page 115
Answers may vary.
People say there's nothing like a bird's-eye view. But people have a hard time getting a bird's-eye view if they don't have wings—unless they go up in a hot-air balloon like I did last weekend. My dad and brother were with me, and my brother loved it! Everywhere you looked, it was a beautiful view. We saw an airplane. And a bird landed right on the edge of the balloon's basket. When we came down, the balloon operator even let us wave to some of the people in the fields below. I just wanted to stay until the next time the balloon went back up, but my dad said we had to go. But as my dad helped my brother out of the basket, my dad said it wouldn't be the last time we got to go for a balloon ride.

page 116
a
a
b
a
b

page 117
Answers may vary.

Every autumn, we love to scare ourselves silly at the haunted house.

It seemed like a lot of money to him (almost five hundred dollars), so he was delighted when he received the check.

Isaac M. Singer, who invented the sewing machine, also designed boats.

Nobody liked to stay after school—especially on days when the football team was playing—so everyone was on their best behavior.

Jennifer Bates, who planted the community garden, took baskets of fresh vegetables around to all of the neighbors.

page 118
Answers may vary.
The whole Parker family had just piled into the family car when (they) realized that something was missing. Riley, the family dog, wasn't in his usual place in the very back of the van. (They) couldn't go to the lake without (him.) So (they) all piled back out of the car to look for (him.) Susie got on (her) hands and knees to check under the porch, where Riley liked to dig. Susie's mom checked the cozy pile of clean laundry (she) had just folded, where Riley often liked to nap. Susie's dad walked up and down the block, calling for Riley to come to (him.) And Susie's brother Jimmy ran upstairs to (his) room, where Riley spent most nights guarding (his) bed. Finally, (they) all gave up and returned to the car. There was Riley, right where (he) belonged, on (his) dog seat in the back of the van, just as if (he) had been waiting for (them) all along.

page 119
Answers may vary.
Officer Cornbloom was convinced there was a robber in the neighborhood. (Him) and his partner always heard sounds coming from the abandoned lot. When he got there, (you) could see the place was empty. The sounds never stopped, until he arrived on the spot. It was a real mystery to (he) and his partner, and it almost drove (they) crazy. Then, in the spring, they finally cracked the case. All over the abandoned lot, beautiful flowers sprang up. And the rascally kids who had been planting at night came out and admitted to (they're) "crimes."

page 120
Answers may vary.

As Jen was telling Ann the story, Ann laughed.

The golfer ran the golf cart into the snack stand, but the snack stand was not damaged.

The clown apologized to the lion tamer, but the lion tamer was still angry

As April steered Ginger on the toboggan to the bottom of the hill, Ginger started to scream.

Every time my dad goes to visit my grandfather, my grandfather is happy.

page 122
Answers may vary.

hearing
the study of something
part or half of
10
one who does an activity
good
below

page 123

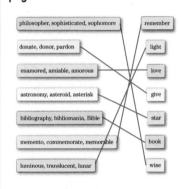

page 124
Answers may vary.

spectacular, spectacle, spectator: look
anniversary, biannual, annual: year
symmetry, sympathy, symbol: with
automobile, automatic, autograph: self
telephone, telegram, telescope: far, end
conform, formation, deform, reform: shape
admire, mirror, miracle: wonder, amazement
antonym, pseudonym, homonym, synonym: name

page 125
Subjective:
I
we
she
he
they

Objective:
me
him
her
them
us

Possessive:
mine
ours
hers
yours
theirs

page 127
adjective
verb
adjective
noun

verb
verb
adjective

page 132
Answers may vary.

It was raining.

The wrestler was big and dangerous.

You make me happy.

It was a bad day.

This tastes delicious.

She's energetic and powerful.

The old door creaked as it swung open.

page 135
Answers may vary.

The economy affects interest rates, wages, and prices in stores. When it gets better, rates go down, wages rise, and prices in stores drop. So when it gets worse, the opposite probably happens.

A hoax involves making a claim that isn't true. It seems to affect more than one person. And falling for a hoax can have big consequences.

Sanctuary is a place where people who have committed crimes or run afoul of powerful leaders can find safety.

When people are intimidated, they might run and hide. People who are intimidated are probably afraid. But the person who is intimidating may not mean to cause fear.

page 136
Answers may vary.

four

$\frac{1}{32}$ of a quart, or $\frac{1}{8}$ of a glass

a place where shale is mined

something valuable found in a quarry under the dirt

a nation

states

page 137
tree frog
lighthouse
clouds
tomatoes
ferns

page 138

page 140
controversy
collaborated
hostile
apprehensive
soothe
knack
resolute

page 141
As soon as I got home, my mother dropped the bomb. No sports for me until my chores were done, even though everybody in the world was already over at the park, playing without me. I was a prisoner in my own home. And let me tell you, she really cracked the whip. I worked like a dog. It took me forever, but I finally finished. Then I raced like a maniac over to the park, just in time to take the last at bat. But what an at bat! The ball went right over the fence and into the Fisher's backyard. I had literally knocked it out of the park.

Answers may vary.

page 144
199,936	92,447	438,414
268,270	114,570	725,718
116,748	452,214	305,900
32,364	86,088	91,840

page 145
3,300	35,492	35,258
3,072	40,096	11,397
14,445	32,996	12,690
65,680		

page 146
157,868	140,514	91,076
114,777	729,400	348,756
454,237	193,960	162,951

page 147
146	561	694
65	6,478	954
582		

page 148
12,173	9,865r4	10,536r1
3,297r6	7,414	4,980r3
17,280r1	7,317	22,117

Captain's extra take: 15

page 149
568	489	657
781	369	742
387	392	603

page 150
83	76	246
588	28	63,375
325		

page 152
12:1, 1, 12
2:4, 2, 4
4:3, 4, 3
2:3, 2, 3
17:11, 17, 11

page 153
17, hour

treats, bag

2, block

3, kid

2, block

page 154
$5
$2
50¢
20¢
$1.25
30¢
75¢

page 155
60 miles per hour
30 laps per hour
500 feet per hour
9 minutes per mile
2 miles per hour

page 156

Farmer Grant
Number of Chickens	Number of Eggs
1	1
2	2
	4
8	8
10	10
15	15
50	50

Farmer Johnson
Number of Chickens	Number of Eggs
1	2
2	4
4	8
8	16
10	20
15	30
50	100

page 157
3:4

5:8

4:16

$\frac{7}{10}$

$\frac{19}{20}$

10:16

Bonus: Yes; #2 and #6

page 158
yes	yes
no	no
no	yes
yes	yes

page 159
12%
36%
32%
85%
75%

page 160
34
15
40
500
150

page 161
The math teacher assigns 2 pages of homework a night. The social studies teacher assigns five times as many pages.

The home team hit 4 home runs. The visiting team hit two and a half times that amount.

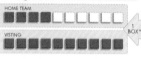

The newspaper staff spent 3 days writing the article. The printer took 21 days to print the issue.

The concert choir raised $1,000 to go on tour. The glee club raised one fifth that amount.

page 162
2.5
126
15

page 163
(2,7)
(7, 30)
(80, 18)
(18, 180)

pages 164–165
6, 5
1, 9
1, 9
3, 3
7, 8
8, 270
3, 70
9, 1
8, 2

page 166
$\frac{1}{100}$

$\frac{1}{16}$

$\frac{1}{3}$

, or $\frac{1}{2}$

6 inches

page 167

4
40
03
6

page 168

SCIENTIST A

OUNCES OF FOOD	NUMBER OF CELLS
1	100
2	200
3	300
4	400
5	500

SCIENTIST B

OUNCES OF FOOD	NUMBER OF CELLS
2	300
4	600
6	900
8	1,200
10	1,500

page 169

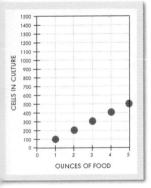

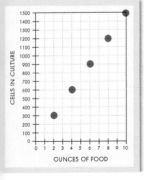

page 170

6
11.66
8
,800

page 172

$\frac{8}{9}$

$\frac{16}{10}$ or $\frac{8}{5}$

$\frac{12}{7}$

$1\frac{1}{4}$

$\frac{5}{16}$

$\frac{3}{2}$ or $1\frac{1}{2}$

$\frac{3}{20}$

page 173

Add:
3.58
35.97
240.43

Subtract:
3.9
10.64
134.9

Multiply:
79.56
232.759
5,207.14

Divide:
41.0
2.15
130.0

page 174

5
6
9
22
24

Bonus: 12

5(1 + 15)
6(4 − 9)
9(8 + 9)
22(1 + 4)
24(2 − 3)

page 175

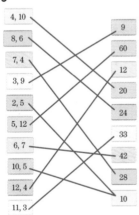

4, 10		9
8, 6		60
7, 4		12
3, 9		20
2, 5		24
5, 12		33
6, 7		42
10, 5		28
12, 4		10
11, 3		

Bonus: 2, 5 and 10, 5

page 176

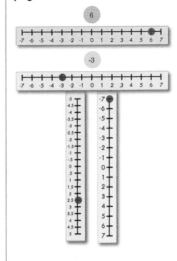

6
−3.5
0.5
70

page 177

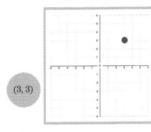 (3, 3)

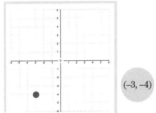 (−3, −4)

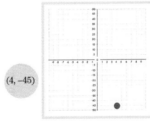 (4, −45)

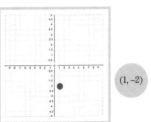 (1, −2)

5; −3
8; 4
−5; 2
−10; -3

page 178

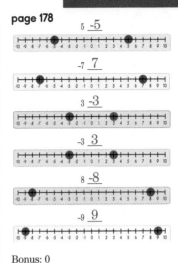

5 −5

-7 7

3 -3

-3 3

8 -8

-9 9

Bonus: 0

page 179

−3, −3

3, −3

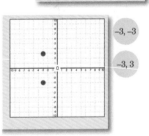

−3, −3

−3, 3

2, −3

−2, 3

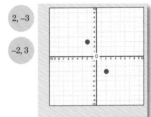

−3, 3

3, −3

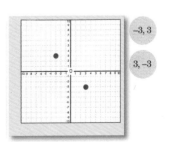

page 171

Bonus: 96 days

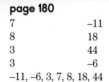

page 180

7	−11
8	18
3	44
3	−6

−11, −6, 3, 7, 8, 18, 44

page 181

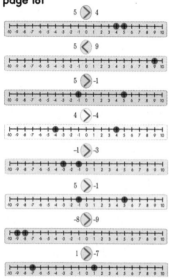

Bonus: the right side

page 182

30 mi. < 35 mi.

50°C > -2°C

1 g > 1 mg

50¢ > 1¢

Twelve ducklings are more than two ducklings.

Fifteen miles per hour is slower than seventy miles per hour.

One gallon is less than 200 gallons.

Three pizzas are more than one pizza.

page 183

14
7
14
7
14
|−1| = 1
|−10| = 10
|−4| = 4

page 184

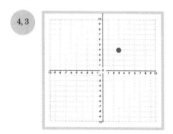

page 185

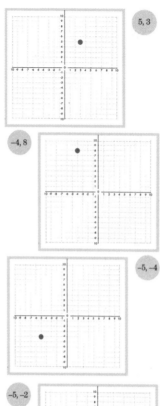

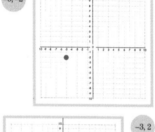

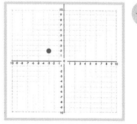

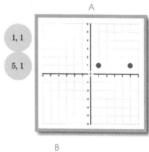

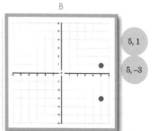

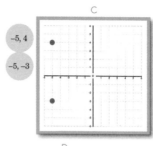

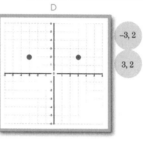

4
4
7
6

page 186

$2 \times 2 \times 2$
$4 \times 4 \times 4 \times 4 \times 4$
10×10
$5 \times 5 \times 5 \times 5 \times 5 \times 5 \times 5$
12^3
125^2
7^5
2^7
1,000
32
10,000
256

page 188

A > B
B + 1 tablespoon = A
2C + D = 1 cup
124
−7
42
0
4,900

page 189

$5 + a$
$b - 10$
$5a$
$\frac{7}{b}$
$a + b$
ab
$5(a + b)$
$\frac{(b + 5)}{a}$

page 190

$(x + y)$
$\left(\frac{y}{x}\right)$
2
5, 3
3
3, ab, $5xy$
5, x, y
2
ab, $5xy$

5
1
2

page 191

630 sq. in.
720 sq. ft.
90 sq. ft.
2.7 pails
1,000 cu. in.
900 cu. in.

page 192

0.12
102.5
480
0.125
16
7
0.625
6,400

page 193

not equivalent
not equivalent
equivalent
not equivalent
not equivalent
equivalent
equivalent

page 195

Month	Ribs	Cole Slaw	Iced Tea
January	204	10	2
February	267	9	3
March	325	8	7
April	375	7	7
May	408	5	8
June	440	5	10
July	518	4.5	10
August	650	4	11
September	395	6	9
October	401	6	9
November	451	5	8
December	793	3	13

page 196

December
December
January
January
fewer
more

page 197

$10x$
$8bc$
$ab + 2$
$xy + 2$

page 198

15
273
$11x + 110$
$3y + 2x + 3$
$24x + 32y$
$11x$
$x^2 + xy$
$40x + 4x^2 + 4xy$
$63x + 27y + 45 + 9z^3$

page 199

5 = 7; not true
7 = 7; true

$0 = -5$; not true
$= 2$; not true
$0 = 100$; not true
$= 5$; true
$2 = 12$; true

age 200

et

ingle value

et

ingle value

age 201

$+ 2x = y$ $7 + (2 \times 7) = y$ $y = 21$
$y = z$ $2 \times 30 = z$ $z = 60$
$+ (x + 3) = y$ $15 +$
$15 + 3) = y$ $y = 33$
$y = z$ $55 \times 7 = z$ $z =$
85

age 202

$= 2y$
$= y + 1$
$= 60y$
$= 3y$

age 203

Shaunte	Cherise
2 mph	1 mph
4 mph	2 mph
6 mph	3 mph
8 mph	4 mph

Tim	Jasper
1 push-up	2 push-ups
5 push-ups	6 push-ups
7 push-ups	8 push-ups
10 push-ups	11 push-ups

Hours	Miles
1	60
2	120
3	180
5	300

Hours	Glasses of Water
1	3
2	6
3	9
4	12

age 204

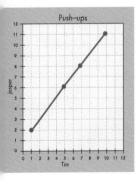

Speed (mph)

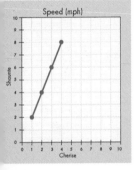

Push-ups

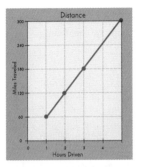

Distance

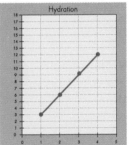

Hydration

Bonus: x-axis: Hours Practiced,
y-axis: Glasses Drunk

page 206

area = 9 sq. in.
volume = 13.5 cu. in.

area = 50 sq. in.
volume = 350 cu. in.

area = 88 sq. in.
volume = 264 cu. in.

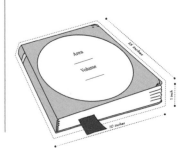

area = 150 sq. in.
volume = 150 cu. in.

page 207

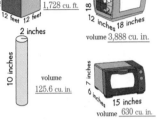

area 49 sq. in.

area 120 sq. ft.

area 28 sq. ft.

volume 1,728 cu. ft.

volume 3,888 cu. in.

volume 125.6 cu. in.

volume 630 cu. in.

Bonus: 52.5 cu. ft.

page 208
231 sq. ft.
90 cu. ft.
No
450 cubic feet
Bonus: 388,800

page 209

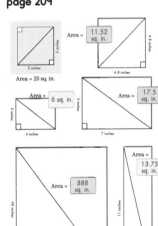

Area = 25 sq. in.

Area = 11.52 sq. in.

Area = 6 sq. in.

Area = 17.5 sq. in.

Area = 888 sq. in.

Area = 13.75 sq. in.

Area = 4 sq. in.

page 210

12
120

page 211

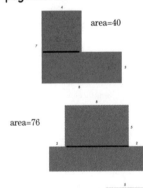

pages 212–213
331 sq. yd.; $x = 13$ yd.
103 sq. yd.; $x = 2$ yd.
80.5 sq. yd.; $x = 9$ yd.
53 sq. yd.; $y = 5$ yd.; $x = 5$ yd.
40 sq. yd.; $y = 1.5$

page 214
$\frac{1}{2}(17 \times 22)$
187 sq. ft.
two rectangles
$(24 \times 15) + (3 \times 6)$
378 sq. ft.

page 215
two rectangles
$(6 \times 8) - (3 \times 1.5)$
43.5 sq. ft.
two rectangles and a triangle
$(24 \times 1.5) + \left(\frac{1.5 \times 1.5}{2}\right) + (11 \times 1.5)$
53.625 square inches

page 216–217

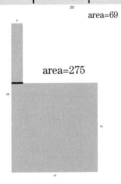

area=40

area=76

area=69

area=275

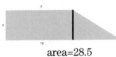

area=28.5

page 218

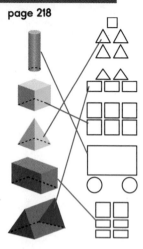

page 219

4 books
8 layers
32 books
No; 14 books
176 cubic inches
5,632 cubic inches
5,632 cubic inches
They are equal.

page 220–221

8.75 cubic inches
2.5 inches
4 candy bars
3 candy bars
12 candy bars
9.5 inches
1,995 cubic inches
22.5 feet
12 boxes
18 feet
14,580 cubic feet
648 cartons
886,464 candy bars

page 224   1

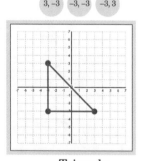

shape: Triangle

2

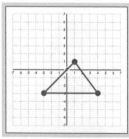

shape: Triangle

3

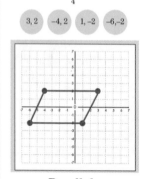

shape: Trapezoid

4

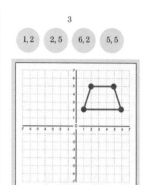

shape: Parallelogram

page 222–223

A
B,D
C
D
A

Bonus: #2

page 226

B
A
neither
A
both

page 227

Everyone on the block

As many answers as there are people on the block

Yes

Mrs. Singh

1

No

Everyone on the block

As many answers as there are people on the block

Yes

page 228

Chocolate
Vanilla
18
12
Rocky road
Saturday

page 229

Saturday
Monday

Monday, Tuesday, and Wednesday
Friday, Saturday, and Sunday
Friday

page 230

12, 13

23 cones

8 years

It curves downward, steeply at first and then more gently.

3:00

25

3:00

22 cones

It moves upward, peaks, and moves downward again.

page 231

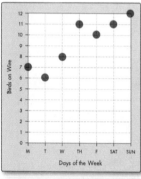

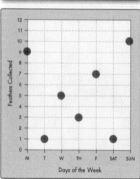

page 233

22
38
16
50
44%

page 234

red
all the women were wearing red scarves at the coffee shop
50%

Red: 11
Blue: 22
Green: 6
Yellow: 11
twice as popular

page 235

Answers may vary.

They are the closest to the event. They are easy to access.

They might pretend they've done more or less homework than they

have. They may not have paid attention to how long it took them to do their homework.

The teacher keeps good records of things like grades. The teacher knows the students well.

The teacher was not there while the homework was being done. The teacher may have preconceptions about the students that cloud the data.

The family likely observed the homework being done. The family may have less reason to give inaccurate data than the student does.

It's more trouble to talk to the family than to the students. The family may not have been paying attention to the homework being done, so they may know less than the student.

The data may be more accurate. There is no one between the surveyor and the data.

It's a challenge to measure all the homework. Even the surveyor may take inaccurate measurements.

page 236

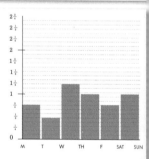

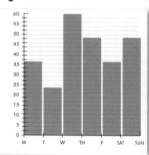

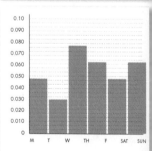

Bonus: You can choose whichever you like, but cups may provide the easiest numbers to work with.

Page 237

6
77
,476
46

8 problems per day
miles per day

age 238

7

41
00
50
90
5
,232
6
1

age 239

, 1, 4, 7, (9), 13, 14, 25, 26
5, 38, 39, 40, 41, (42), 75, 77, 85, 96, 01

5, 25, 27, 28, (28), 30, 31, 36, 37

05, 256, (289), 352, 1835, 12

age 240

0%

age 241

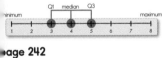

age 242

enter
enter
ariability

ages 244–245

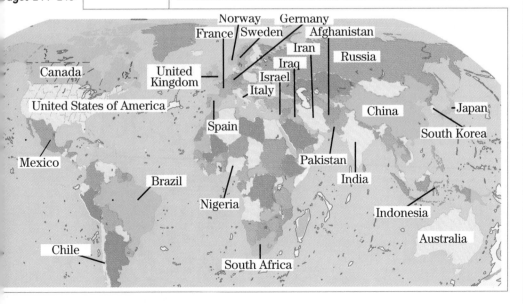

page 247

Answers may vary.

It is an administration that favors the many instead of the few.
social standing, poverty
fear

laws on the statute book, unwritten code

page 249

unlimited
limited
unlimited
unlimited
limited

pages 250–251

4
3
1
7
6
2
5

page 252

80 years
52 years
96 years
women

Answers may vary depending on what year you use this book.

page 255

1) establishment of religion
2) free exercise of religion
3) freedom of speech
4) freedom of the press
5) peaceful assembly
6) petition the government for a redress of grievances

1) keep arms
2) bear arms

1) unreasonable search
2) unreasonable seizure

1) a speedy trial
2) a public trial
3) an impartial jury

pages 256–257

Mexico City—Mexico
Berlin—German
Moscow—Russia
Shanghai—China
New York City—United States of America
Istanbul—Turkey
Sydney—Australia
Rio de Janeiro—Brazil
Rome—Italy

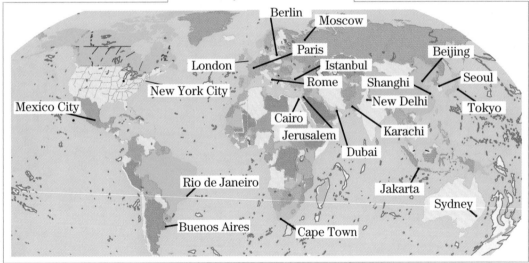

Beijing—China
Cairo—Egypt
Paris—France
Cape Town—South Africa
Jerusalem—Israel
London—United Kingdom
Dubai—United Arab Emirates
Tokyo—Japan
Jakarta—Indonesia
Seoul—South Korea
Karachi—Pakistan
New Delhi—India
Buenos Aires—Argentina

page 259

Answers may vary.
no
It's bad to live in cities.
It's good to live in cities.
anything good about living in cities
anything bad about living in cities

page 261

that the place was half empty

Sharon says the ring was on her left hand; A. J. says the ring was on her right hand.

Jesse says he was there; Sharon says he wasn't.

proving he was there at an important event

how nervous the singer was; and that the show wasn't good until the end

page 263

Answers may vary.

1) the date of the show

2) the name of the singer

3) the name of the club

4) the location of the club

Most people don't usually mention dates and proper names in conversation.

The club was half empty.

Sharon uses a nickname: Joe's.

Probably not; they didn't seem to realize it was such an important show.

page 265
no
Australia
100 percent
North America

page 267
OK: Fair Use
OK: Open Source
OK: Creative Commons
Get Permission: Fair Use

OK; Public Domain

page 269
billions

They all use the TCP/IP protocol.

Your computer connects with another computer.

anyone who wants to and has the equipment

page 270

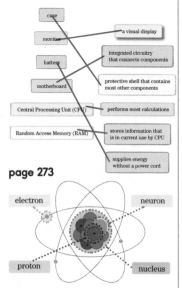

page 273

atom
electron
electron

page 274
renewable
nonrenewable
nonrenewable
nonrenewable
renewable
renewable

page 275
Step 2
Step 1
Step 3
Step 4

pages 276–277

E	S	J	Q	N
L	H	M	I	K
B	C	P	R	D
O	T	F	G	A

page 279
5 percent

1 percent

in glaciers

Rain carries minerals and salt into the oceans.

about half

page 281
wind, rotation of earth, shape of shore, temperature, saltiness

moon and sun

wind, disturbances under water, disturbances on land

cold, salty water

the sun

page 282

page 283
nuclear membrane
endoplasmic reticulum
nucleus
cytoplasm
cell membrane

Bonus: likely a plant cell, because very few animal cells contain chlorophyll

page 285
oxygen
Fe
8
7
18
about sixteen times more mass

page 287
100°C
32°F
180°
100°
98.6°F
32°F

page 288
potential
both
kinetic
potential
both

page 289
1) observation
2) hypothesis
3) experiment
4) analyze
5) accept or reject hypothesis

Brain Quest
Extras

Congratulations!

You've finished the Brain Quest Workbook!
In this section, you'll find:

Brain Quest Mini-Deck

Cut out the cards and make your own Brain Quest deck.

Play by yourself or with a friend.

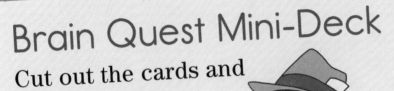

Brainiac Certificate

Finish the whole workbook, and you're an official Brainiac!

QUESTIONS

 ENGLISH — Who is the author of *Tom Sawyer*?

How many people were part of the British Empire at its height? **SOCIAL STUDIES**

 SCIENCE — If an element has an atomic number of 17, how many protons does it have in its nucleus?

What part of the word "production" is a prefix? **ENGLISH**

QUESTIONS

 MATH — Is an *x*-axis horizontal or vertical?

What did a young Frederick Douglass trade for his reading lessons?

 ENGLISH — Is "they" a noun or a pronoun?

Would the point (-5, -5) be above or below the *x*-axis on a graph? **MATH**

QUESTIONS

 SCIENCE — What kind of membrane surrounds an entire cell?

What is the largest state in the United States? **GEOGRAPHY**

 SOCIAL STUDIES — What city did Pericles live in?

Is 10 > or < 25? **MATH**

QUESTIONS

 ENGLISH — If there are sixteen ounces in a pound, what fraction of a pound is an ounce?

Which amendment to the United States Constitution establishes freedom of religion? **SOCIAL STUDIES**

 GEOGRAPHY — Is "we" a singular or plural pronoun??

What side of the number line does the largest number appear on, right or left? **MATH**

ANSWERS

horizontal

bread

pronoun

below

ANSWERS

Mark Twain

460 million

17

pro

ANSWERS

$\frac{1}{16}$

the First Amendment

Plural

right

ANSWERS

Cell membrane

Alaska

Athens

<

QUESTIONS

 Who is the author of *Little Women*?

What is the greatest common factor of 21, 63, and 70?

 What kind of pronouns add emphasis to a sentence?

How far away from zero is –5 on the number line?

QUESTIONS

 What is the volume of a box that is 1 foot high, 2 feet wide, and 3 feet deep?

Is an eyewitness of an event a primary or a secondary source?

 Which of these numbers is a deviation in the data: 2, 3, 2, 4, 1, 3, 25?

What is colder, 0°K or 0°C?

QUESTIONS

 Would a temperature below zero be measured in negative or positive numbers?

What is the word for an idea or feeling a word gives us, along with its main meaning?

 In an equation, can the value of a variable change?

What do we find when we use the formula "length × width × height"?

QUESTIONS

 What is a word that takes the place of a noun?

In what year did the United States pass the Civil Rights Act?

 In what quadrant of the coordinate plane would this point be: (3, –3)?

Do we get a sum by multiplying or adding numbers?

310

ANSWERS

 6 cubic feet

primary

 25

0°K

ANSWERS

 Louisa May Alcott

7

 intensive pronouns

5

ANSWERS

 a pronoun

1964

 bottom right

adding

ANSWERS

 negative

connotation

 yes

volume

QUESTIONS

 MATH There are ten tigers and eleven lions. What is the ratio of tigers to lions?

What kind of pronouns refer back to a subject that was mentioned earlier? **ENGLISH**

 SCIENCE Are tides caused by the moon and sun, by wind, or by the temperature of sea water?

What is the absolute value of 3? **MATH**

QUESTIONS

 GEOGRAPHY What lakes contain 21% of all the fresh water on the surface of the planet?

Is "he" a first person, second person, or third person pronoun? **ENGLISH**

 ENGLISH What kind of figurative language exaggerates in order to capture attention?

What is the lowest common denominator of $\frac{1}{2}$, $\frac{4}{8}$, and $\frac{3}{6}$? **MATH**

QUESTIONS

 MATH Are A^3 and $3A$ equivalent?

What do we call the word or idea that a pronoun replaces? **ENGLISH**

 ENGLISH What does the root "spec," as in spectacle or spectator, mean?

What is the absolute value of |-8|? **MATH**

QUESTIONS

 ENGLISH Will a sentence still make sense if we take out a nonrestrictive element?

If we multiply both sides of an equation by 5, will the equation still be equal? **MATH**

 SOCIAL STUDIES What group of people did the 19th amendment give the right to vote?

If three equally priced candy bars add up to $1.50, what does one candy bar cost? **MATH**

312

ANSWERS

 GEOGRAPHY the Great Lakes

third person ENGLISH

 ENGLISH hyperbole

$\frac{1}{2}$ MATH

ANSWERS

 MATH 10:11

reflexive pronouns ENGLISH

 SCIENCE the moon and sun

3 MATH

ANSWERS

 ENGLISH yes

yes MATH

 SOCIAL STUDIES women

50 cents MATH

ANSWERS

 MATH no

antecedent  ENGLISH

 ENGLISH to see

8 MATH

QUESTIONS

 MATH What do we call a variable that changes when another variable changes?

What were scientists trying to improve when they accidentally invented the microwave oven? **SCIENCE**

 ENGLISH What part of speech is the word "priority"?

If x = 9, is x < 8? **MATH**

QUESTIONS

 SOCIAL STUDIES What was the largest city in the world in 200 CE?

When we guess a word's meaning based on how another person uses it, what are we using? **ENGLISH**

 MATH This formula calculates the area of which shape: $\frac{1}{2}$ (length of leg × length of leg)

How many sides does a cube have? **MATH**

QUESTIONS

 SOCIAL STUDIES Who talked Thomas Jefferson into writing the Declaration of Independence?

What does the affix "astr," as in asteroid or astronomy, mean? **ENGLISH**

 MATH Is 6:8 equivalent to 8:10?

What is the area of a wall that is 10 feet high and 8 feet wide? **MATH**

QUESTIONS

 ENGLISH What do we call it when someone steals another person's words or ideas?

What continent is Australia on? **GEOGRAPHY**

 GEOGRAPHY What percent of the world's water is not in an ocean?

What is the shape of the four sides of a pyramid? **MATH**

ANSWERS

 Rome

context

 a right triangle

6

ANSWERS

 dependent

radar

 noun

no

ANSWERS

 plagiarism

Australia

 3.5%

triangle

ANSWERS

 John Adams

star

 no

80 square feet

315

QUESTIONS

 Do statistical questions require one single answer or many answers to answer a question?
MATH

What do we look at when we want to know more about the source of a piece of information?
ENGLISH

 What does the pronunciation of a word tell us?
ENGLISH

How many sides does a rhombus have?
MATH

QUESTIONS

 What does the mean absolute deviation describe?
MATH

What is the most populous city in the world today?
GEOGRAPHY

 What part of speech is "conspicuously"?
ENGLISH

What is the product of $\frac{1}{3}$ multiplied by $\frac{1}{2}$?
MATH

QUESTIONS

 Are 14xy + 2x and 2(7xy + x) equivalent?
MATH

Is coal a renewable resource?
SCIENCE

 What is the title of Robert Louis Stevenson's famous book about pirates?
ENGLISH

If a = 3, what is $3a + \frac{1}{3}a$?
MATH

QUESTIONS

 What percent of the world's population lives under some form of democracy today?
SOCIAL STUDIES

What did young Frederick Douglass desire more than anything else?
SOCIAL STUDIES

 Does a simile or a metaphor use the words "like" or "as"?
ENGLISH

Does an interquartile range concentrate on data in the middle of a set, or on the highest and lowest ranges?
MATH

ANSWERS

 MATH — the distance of each point of data in a set from the mean

Shanghai GEOGRAPHY

 ENGLISH — adverb

$\frac{1}{6}$ MATH

ANSWERS

 MATH — many

the citation ENGLISH

 ENGLISH — how to say it aloud

4 MATH

ANSWERS

 SOCIAL STUDIES — over half

freedom SOCIAL STUDIES

 ENGLISH — simile

the middle of a set MATH

ANSWERS

 MATH — yes

no SCIENCE

 ENGLISH — *Treasure Island*

10 MATH

QUESTIONS

 MATH 20 of the school's 50 students walk to school. What percentage of the students walk to school?

Does a histogram display data in dots or bars? **MATH**

 ENGLISH If a narrator refers to herself as "I," is the story in first or second person?

Does a proton have a positive or a negative charge? **SCIENCE**

QUESTIONS

 ENGLISH What book by H. G. Wells begins when a man finds a crashed spaceship?

Hector runs a mile in 10 minutes. How many miles can he run in half an hour? **MATH**

 ENGLISH What do we call language that is only used in a certain field?

What do we find by adding all the terms in a series, then dividing the sum by the number of terms? **MATH**

QUESTIONS

 ENGLISH Who wrote *The Secret Garden*?

If a book was written two hundred years ago, is it still under copyright? **SOCIAL STUDIES**

 ENGLISH What do we call it when we imagine that objects have thoughts or feelings?

What do we call the range from the highest to the lowest point of data? **MATH**

QUESTIONS

 GEOGRAPHY What continent is Pakistan on?

What language do computer networks use to communicate on the Internet? **SCIENCE**

 SOCIAL STUDIES Was Socrates a general, a philosopher, or a king?

If there are 8 ounces in a glass of milk, and 128 ounces in a gallon, how many glasses are in a gallon? **MATH**

318

ANSWERS

 ENGLISH *War of the Worlds*

three MATH

 ENGLISH jargon

the mean MATH

ANSWERS

 MATH 40%

bars MATH

 ENGLISH first person

positive SCIENCE

ANSWERS

 GEOGRAPHY Asia

Internet protocol suite, TCP/IP SCIENCE

 SOCIAL STUDIES a philosopher

16 MATH

ANSWERS

 ENGLISH Frances Hodgson Burnett

no SOCIAL STUDIES

 ENGLISH personification

spread MATH

Brainiac Award!

You have completed the entire Brain Quest Workbook! Woo-hoo! Congratulations! That's quite an achievement.

Write your name on the line and cut out the award certificate.

Show your friends. Hang it on your wall! You're a certified Brainiac!

Brainiac Award

BRAIN QUEST

Presented to:

_____

for successfully completing all fourteen chapters of

BRAIN QUEST 6TH GRADE WORKBOOK

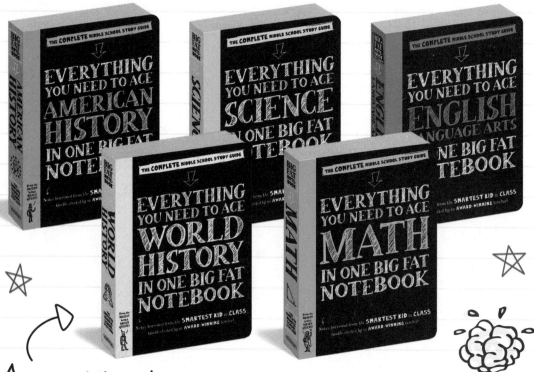